A MAINE
COOKBOOK

A compilation of 150 years of
cooking in the best Yankee tradition

Lithographed by
Twin City Printery, Inc., Lewiston, Maine

INTRODUCTION

Maine, land of rugged seas and stately pines, boasts a colorful heritage of New England cooking.

This cookbook depicts Maine's growth in the culinary art. Many of the recipes have delighted generations of Down Easterners having been handed down from mother to daughter and are now presented to you for your dining pleasure.

Tourists from all over the world come to this great state every year to enjoy an unspoiled land and to savor many of the recipes found on these pages.

Complete sections have been devoted to Maine's specialties: lobster, clams, fish and potatoes. You'll find special chowders and many other out of the ordinary taste-tested recipes to tempt the most discriminating palate.

Truly a combination of the old and the new: one hundred and fifty years of Maine cooking in the true Down East tradition awaits you in the pages ahead.

TABLE OF CONTENTS

MAINE, LAND OF SEA AND PINES

From the low lands of Kittery and York to the heights of Mt. Desert and Quoddy Head, Maine presents the most remarkable coast in the western hemisphere. The coasts and forest of this great state have their own individual charms, yet there are parts which suggest the glory of other lands: Bar Harbor is of the Mediterranean, the Aegean; Casco Bay, a Bermuda of the North; Moosehead is of the Swiss Lakes, the Penobscot is an American Rhone River, lacking the feudal castles, the terraced vineyards, yet more lovely with all in her wildness, her naturalness; Aroostook is of the West of wheat, and rolling plains and limitless cultivation; and Katahdin, the lonely lord of the woods.

Glooskap rules over the sea and the coast, over the woods and the mountains; Glooskap, the Great Spirit, whose children still linger at Old Town and Pleasant Point, conquered all. These legends of the Indian are not among the least of Maine's charm. Each island has its story, each headland and bay a romance. A sea-yarn is on the lips of every fisherman and lobsterman.

To these bays and inlets belong the history and romance of the French and English. It is the story of the explorer, the adventurer; and to the shores are attached the names of Cabot, of Captain John Smith, Miles Standish, Sieur de Monts, Champlain, Arnold, and Burr. The misty legends of Marie Antoinette and of Talleyrand give a touch of the weird to the coast land. Here was the historical beginning of New England.

Crab Flake Cocktail

5 well-shaped green peppers	6 tablespoons catsup
6 tablespoons lemon juice	1 tablespoon horseradish
¼ teaspoon curry powder	¼ teaspoon Worcestershire
1¼ cups crab flakes cut in inch lengths	Lettuce hearts

Cut peppers in half, crosswise, scraping out seeds and core. Rinse in cold water, dry and fill with a sauce made of catsup, lemon juice, curry powder, horseradish and Worcestershire. Place on a bed of lettuce hearts, arrange on individual plates and dispose the flakes on the leaves around the base of each cup.

Baked Oysters on the Half Shell

Allow 6 oysters per person. Place the oysters on the half shell in a dripping pan. Place a small strip of bacon on each oyster and bake in moderate oven until oysters curl (about 5 minutes). Serve garnished with a slice of lemon decorated with strips of pimento, gringed celery and parsley.

Clam and Grapefruit Cocktail

24 little neck clams
Sections from 2 grapefruits
2 tablespoons shredded
  red and green peppers
1 tablespoon lemon juice
½ teaspoon salt
Dash tobasco
Grated orange rind
¼ teaspoon Worcestershire
Few grains curry powder

Wash the clams thoroughly. Cut the sections from the grapefruit and separate into 4 pieces each. Put the ingredients together in a bowl, mix, cover and chill thoroughly. Serve in lemon or green pepper cups.

Scallop Cocktail

¾ teaspoon chopped
  parsley
1 teaspoon scraped onion
1 teaspoon olive oil
10 drops tobasco sauce
1 teaspoon Worcestershire
1½ cups small scallops
6 green peppers or
  hollowed tomato cups
1 teaspoon salt
1 teaspoon mustard
2 tablespoons vinegar
½ cup tomato catsup
1 tablespoon grated
  horseradish

Cook scallops for five minutes in salted boiling water. Drain, chill and halve them. Mix together remainder of ingredients, add the scallops and divide in six portions into the cups.

Oyster Cocktail (Individual)

6 small raw oysters
½ tablespoon tomato catsup
¼ tablespoon vinegar or
  lemon juice
Grated orange rind
1 drop tobasco

Dash of salt
1 teaspoon celery,
  chopped fine
¼ teaspoon fine
  Worcestershire

Mix the ingredients in the order given, chill thoroughly and serve.

Hot Oyster Canapes

1½ cups cream
4 tablespoons fine soft
  bread crumbs
1½ tablespoons butter
Few grains red pepper
Few grains nutmeg

Toast rounds
24 oysters (cut in halves)
2 tablespoons minced
  peppers
¾ cup quartered
  mushrooms

Melt butter and add mushrooms and peppers and saute until softened. Add cream, crumbs and seasonings. When hot, add oysters. Stir until the edges begin to curl, then serve on well-buttered toast rounds.

Grapefruit and Tomato Cocktail

2 tablespoons chopped tomato
1 tablespoon shredded grapefruit pulp
½ tablespoon lemon juice
Dash salt and pepper

1 teaspoon olive oil
2 teaspoons minced green peppers
Grapefruit juice and mayonnaise to moisten thoroughly

Combine and serve.

Vegetable Cocktails

CUCUMBER COCKTAIL (Individual)

2 tablespoons chopped cucumber
1 teaspoon grated horseradish

1 tablespoon minced celery
1 teaspoon minced chives
1 teaspoon minced radishes

Put together with a little strong celery stock, a dash of salt and pepper and mayonnaise or sour cream salad dressing to moisten. Chill for one hour.

Oyster Cocktail (Individual)

6 small raw oysters
½ tablespoon tomato catsup
¼ tablespoon vinegar or
   lemon juice
Grated orange rind
1 drop tobasco

Dash of salt
1 teaspoon celery,
   chopped fine
¼ teaspoon fine
   Worcestershire

Mix the ingredients in the order given, chill thoroughly and serve.

Hot Oyster Canapes

1½ cups cream
4 tablespoons fine soft
   bread crumbs
1½ tablespoons butter
Few grains red pepper
Few grains nutmeg

Toast rounds
24 oysters (cut in halves)
2 tablespoons minced
   peppers
¾ cup quartered
   mushrooms

Melt butter and add mushrooms and peppers and saute until softened. Add cream, crumbs and seasonings. When hot, add oysters. Stir until the edges begin to curl, then serve on well-buttered toast rounds.

Mushroom Canapes

6 round bread crousades	2 tablespoons thick cream
6 large mushrooms	3 tablespoons minced ham
1 tablespoon butter	1 tablespoon green
Salt and pepper	pepper, minced
Nutmeg — sprinkling	

Prepare 6 shallow bread croustades and either toast or fry them. Remove skins from the mushrooms and scoop out gills. Chop stems, add peppers and saute in butter until softened. Add cream and ham season and pile lightly into inverted mushroom caps. Bake 5 minutes in a quick oven, set in the croustades and serve individually.

Sardine Celery Sticks

Select tender celery; trim the ends square and fill the grooves with sardine paste made according to the proportions given for making tuna fish balls only substitute sardines for the tuna fish. Chill and cut in two-inch strips.

Tuna Fish Cocktail, in Orange Cups (Individual)

6 large flakes tuna fish
¼ tablespoon lemon juice
½ teaspoon grated
   horseradish
1 drop tobasco

½ tablespoon grapefruit
   juice
Grated orange rind
Few grains celery salt

Mix sauce ingredients together, scoop out halves of small oranges and line with fringed wax paper. Pour in the sauce and add the tuna fish. Place individually on doily-covered plate, surround with tiny parsley sprigs and sprinkle with minced parsley. Use the orange pulp for a shortcake or orange jelly.

Aspic Cocktail

2 tablespoons minced
   tomato
1 tablespoon minced celery
1 tablespoon aspic jelly
   cut in bits

½ teaspoon pickled chives
Few drops tobasco sauce
French dressing and
   mayonnaise to moisten
   thoroughly

Combine and serve.

Grapefruit and Tomato Cocktail

2 tablespoons chopped
   tomato
1 tablespoon shredded
   grapefruit pulp
½ tablespoon lemon juice
Dash salt and pepper

1 teaspoon olive oil
2 teaspoons minced green
   peppers
Grapefruit juice and
   mayonnaise to moisten
   thoroughly

Combine and serve.

Vegetable Cocktails

CUCUMBER COCKTAIL (Individual)

2 tablespoons chopped
   cucumber
1 teaspoon grated
   horseradish

1 tablespoon minced celery
1 teaspoon minced chives
1 teaspoon minced
   radishes

Put together with a little strong celery stock, a dash of salt and
pepper and mayonnaise or sour cream salad dressing to moisten.
Chill for one hour.

Peanut Butter Canapes

6 buttered toast rounds
Peanut butter
Narrow strips of green
 and red peppers

Thick mayonnaise dressing
 or well moistened
 cream cheese

Spread the toast rounds lightly with peanut butter and place alternately on them the strips of red and green peppers pressing firmly into place. Pipe the mayonnaise or cream cheese around the edge by means of a pastry bag and tube.

Tomato Canapes

6 slices bread
6 slices tomato
½ Neufchatel cheese
Stiff mayonnaise

Salt, pepper and paprika
2 tablespoons powdered
 parsley

Cut 6 slices of bread in round shapes and toast and fry. Spread lightly with well-seasoned cream cheese and set over it a slice of tomato. Sprinkle with salt and pepper. Pipe around each tomato slice a ring of mayonnaise, studded with mayonnaise roses and pile three tiny balls of cream cheese, rolled in parsley on each tomato slice.

THE DISCOVERY OF MAINE

Glooskap, the Great Spirit was responsible for the discovery of Maine. When he was a boy he worked a year to build a stone canoe. He provisioned it with moose, deer and fish; and filled seal bladders with water. With his adopted mother the Woodchuck he set sail for the old World from the shores of Maine.

The buffalo skin sails caught the North Wind and carried him to England where he was paid great respect and departed with presents. And he went to the shores of France where men-of-war bombarded his canoe. But the balls could not harm the stone of the Maine coast, and Glooskap picked up the French fleet and threw it on the shore.

Then he took the Woodchuck and went on land. The French took him prisoner and put him in a great cannon. The gun was discharged, and when they looked into the mouth of the cannon, there sat Glooskap, smiling and smoking his pipe. Then they took him to see the great French king. Glooskap told him he had brought his foster mother to France to be baptized, and the French baptized her under the name of Molly. And unto this day all woodchucks are called Molly by the Indians.

The king went with Glooskap to the shore where the Great Spirit picked up the fleet he had thrown ashore and replaced them in the water.

At last, longing to be in the woods, Glooskap and the Woodchuck entered the stone canoe, hoisted the buffalo sails and came home. The French and Englishmen then believed that a great country was in the West. Soon they set sail and came to the realm of Glooskap. To this day the Indians still say that gave Maine to the world.

Tuna Fish Balls

¾ cup tuna fish, pounded	I tablespoon minced
I tablespoon finely	capers
minced chow chow	Stiff mayonnaise
½ tablespoon lemon juice	Powdered parsley

Mix together the first five ingredients with enough mayonnaise to make them adherent; form into small balls and roll in the parsley. Use as an hors-d'oeuvre.

Sardines, Italian Style

For each serving allow:

I canned pimento	2 sardines
¼ of a shredded green	I slice of lemon
pepper	

Lay the pimento on a small plate and place two sardines upon it. Sprinkle with pepper and top with the lemon slice covered lightly with minced parsley. Try a small amount of olive oil with the lemon.

Maine Sardine Cocktail, Machias

1 cup sour cream	Salt and pepper to taste
½ cup seeded and minced cucumber*	3 cans (4 oz. ea) Maine sardines
5 radishes, minced	1 clove garlic, minced
2 scallions, minced	French dressing
½ teaspoon Worcestershire	Lettuce
Dash of cayenne or tabasco	Lemon Wedges
1 tablespoon lemon juice	

Mix sour cream with minced vegetables and seasonings. Chill. Drain Maine sardines and place in shallow dish, taking care not to break them. Sprinkle with minced garlic and cover with a favorite French dressing. Marinate in refrigerator for several hours. To serve, arrange lettuce leaves in chilled cocktail or sherbet glasses. Spoon a tablespoon or so of sour cream dressing into each glass. Drain sardines and divide equally between glasses. Top with additional sour cream dressing and garnish with lemon wedges. Serve ice cold (6 servings).

* Cucumbers should be squeezed dry between paper towels.

Courtesy of Batten, Barton, Durstine & Osborn, Inc.

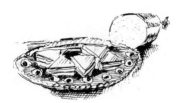

Blue Cheese-Bologna Wedges

1/3 cup crumbled Blue cheese	6 slices Bologna sausage
2 tablespoons cream cheese	12 pimiento-stuffed olives

Blend together blue cheese and cream cheese. Spread 1 tablespoon mixture on each of 5 bologna slices; stack and top with remaining slice. Chill. At serving time, cut into 12 wedges; garnish with pimiento-stuffed olive secured with wooden pick.

Courtesy of American Dairy Assoc.

Clam Cocktail (Individual)

6 little neck clams
½ tablespoon lemon juice
½ teaspoon grated
   horseradish
1 drop tobasco

½ tablespoon grapefruit
   juice
1 tablespoon tomato catsup
Few drops Worcestershire
¼ teaspoon celery salt
Few grains curry powder

Discard the hard heads of clams and wash carefully to remove any grit. Mix the sauce ingredients together, add clams, cover and let stand one hour in a cold place before serving.

Cheese Log

1¼ cups unblanched almonds
½ pound cheddar cheese
1 package (3 oz.) cream
   cheese
1 teaspoon lemon juice

1 teaspoon Worcestershire
1 teaspoon grated onion
½ teaspoon salt
Crackers

Preheat oven 350°. Toast almonds in oven for 10 minutes; allow to cool; chop ¼ cup and set aside. Grind together 1 cup almonds, Cheddar cheese and cream cheese. Add lemon juice, Worcestershire sauce, onion and salt; blend thoroughly. Shape into log approximately 8-inches long and 2-inches in diameter; roll in ¼ cup chopped almonds. Wrap in moisture proof wrap; chill. Slice and serve on crackers.

Courtesy American Dairy Assoc.

Green Pepper Cheese Broil

Bread
2 strips bacon, cut up
¼ cup butter
2 packages (3 oz. ea.) cream cheese
¼ teaspoon garlic salt

1 egg, slightly beaten
3 tablespoons finely chopped green pepper
Cherry tomatoes
Pimiento-stuffed olives

Preheat broiler. Trim crusts from bread; cut into squares, rectangles or circles. Toast one side; set aside. Meanwhile fry bacon until crisp; drain on absorbent paper. Cream together butter and cream cheese until well blended; add garlic salt. Gradually add egg; beat until mixture holds its shape. Fold in green pepper and bacon. (Yield: 1½ cups.) Mound on untoasted sides of bread; top with slices of tomato or olives. Broil 2-3 minutes or until lightly browned on baking sheet.

Courtesy American Dairy Assoc.

Surprise Dip (1¾ cups)

1 package (8 oz.) cream cheese
¾ cup ground or finely minced radishes

½ teaspoon onion salt
¼ cup cut up green onion tops
Potato chips or crackers

In a mixing bowl beat cream cheese until smooth; gradually add radishes. Blend in onion salt and onion tips. Chill. Serve with chips or crackers.

Courtesy American Dairy Assoc.

Deviled Deckers

1 can (4½ oz.) deviled ham

2 teaspoons grated onion

2 cups (½ lb.) shredded Swiss cheese

12 slices day-old bread

Preheat oven 450°. In a small bowl blend together ham, cheese and grated onion. Spread on bread to make four triple-decker sandwiches. Trim crusts from each sandwich; cut each into 9 cubes (hold together with wooden picks). Bake 3-5 minutes or until heated through using shallow baking pan. Makes 36 appetizers.

Courtesy American Dairy Assoc.

Blue Cheese Nut Balls

½ cup crumbled Blue cheese

¼ cup butter

½ cup sifted flour

¾ cup finely chopped pecans

Preheat oven 350°. In a bowl cream together chees and butter; beat until light and fluffy. Gradually add flour; blend thoroughly. Blend in ¼ cup pecans. Chill for ease in handling. Shape into balls ¾ to 1-inch in diameter; roll in remaining ½ cup chopped pecans. Place on baking sheet; bake 12-15 minutes on baking sheet. Remove to wire racks to cool. Makes three dozen.

Courtesy American Dairy Assoc.

Hot Cheese Dip

6 slices bacon
1 package (8 oz.) cream cheese
2 cups (½ lb.) shredded Cheddar cheese
6 tablespoons half and half or light cream

1 teaspoon Worcestershire
¼ teaspoon dry mustard
¼ teaspoon onion salt
3 drops tobasco
Unpared Washington apples, cut in wedges
Lemon juice

Cut bacon into ¼-inch slices; saute until crisp; drain on absorbent paper. Meanwhile, in top of double boiler or in heavy saucepan combine cream cheese, Cheddar cheese, half and half, Worcestershire sauce, mustard, onion salt and tobasco. Heat over hot water or oven low heat stirring occasionally until cheese melts and mixture is hot. Add bacon pieces. Use as dip for apple wedges dipped in lemon juice.

Courtesy American Dairy Assoc.

Savory Stuffed Eggs

8 hard-cooked eggs, shelled
6 tablespoons mayonnaise
¼ teaspoon curry powder
¼ cup minced celery

¼ teaspoon salt
1 4¾ oz. can Underwood Chicken Spread
Salt and pepper to taste

Halve eggs lengthwise, carefully remove yolks. Mash only 4 of the yolks, combine with remaining ingredients. Generously refill eggs. Sprinkle lightly with salt and pepper. Cover and chill. Garnish with paprika. Makes 16 halves.

Courtesy Wm. Underwood Co.

Stuffed Brussels Sprouts

Cut center out of raw sprouts, soak in ice water, drain thoroughly, and fill with cottage or cream cheese seasoned with chopped chives and mixed with heavy cream, sweet or sour.

Stuffed Carrot Slices

Scrape large even carrot. Cut off ends and make hole through center with apple corer. Stuff tightly with highly seasoned cream cheese mixed with finely cut chives. Chill until cheese is firm. Cut in ¼-inch slices. Use to garnish tray of canapes.

STUFFED DILL PICKLE. Use large pickle in place of carrot.

Ham or Dried Beef Rolls

Cut thin slices of meat in even pieces. Spread with cream cheese, highly seasoned with prepared mustard, etc. Roll tightly and serve on toothpicks

Celery Bouillon

1 3-pound knuckle of veal	2 quarts water
1 tablespoon salt	½ teaspoon peppercorn
1 onion	1 bay leaf
Outer stalks of celery	

Wipe the meat and cut in small pieces. Put the meat bone, water, seasonings (except salt) and celery, chopped (leaves and all) in the soup kettle and bring gradually to boiling point. Simmer 4 hours, replenishing the water as it evaporates. Add salt after 2 hours of cooking. Strain and let stand until the fat can be removed. Then clear as usual, reheat and add a spoonful of cooked, diced celery to each serving.

Vegetable Bouillon

1 cup chopped carrots	1 cup broth from canned
1 cup chopped turnip	or fresh asparagus
1 cup chopped celery,	2½ quarts water
outside stalks and leaves	1 teaspoon salt
1 cup chopped onions	1 bay leaf (optional)
2 cups strained tomatoes	

Mix all the ingredients, except the salt. Bring to a boil and simmer slowly 3 to 4 hours then strain; there should be about 1 pint of broth. Season with salt. Some thyme and summer savory may be added. Add 1 teaspoon of vegex or a package of George Washington beef broth.

Clear Tomato Soup

1 pint canned tomatoes or sufficent fresh tomatoes to make 1 pint when stewed
1 cup water
½ onion, sliced

1 bit of bay leaf
A few grains of thyme
A few grains of savory
1 teaspoon sugar
1 teaspoon salt

Combine the above and cook 20 minutes. Rub through a fine colander. Reheat and add water to replenish what boils away. Thicken with 2 tablespoons flour rubbed smooth with a little cold water. Add 1 tablespoon butter or oil.

Beef Bouillon

3 pounds lower round of beef
1 sprig parsley
¼ cup finely diced celery or 1 teaspoon celery salt
1 bay leaf

3 cloves
3 quarts cold water
1 onion, minced
1 small carrot, minced
1 tablespoon salt

Cut the meat in inch pieces and let stand in cold water for 1 hour. Cover, bring slowly to boiling point and remove any scum that may arise. Let simmer for 3 hours then add the vegetables, spices and seasonings and simmer 1 hour longer, replenishing the water as necessary to keep the quantity about 2 quarts. Strain, cool, remove the fat and clear the bouillon, as directed.

Tomato Bouillon

1½ quarts water
2 tablespoons minced onion
2 tablespoons minced carrot
1 teaspoon salt

1/8 teaspoon pepper
¼ teaspoon Worcestershire
2 cups canned tomatoes
1 bay leaf
2 teaspoons beef extract or 1 quart beef stock

Combine 2 cups boiling water, onion, carrot and tomato and simmer, uncovered for 20 minutes. Dissolve the extract in a quart of boiling water, add to the tomato mixture, season and put through a fine strainer. To make the bouillon very clear, strain through cheesecloth.

Swedish Cabbage Soup

1 pint finely chopped cabbage
Bit of bay leaf
Few grains mace
1 quart veal stock
Salt and pepper to taste
2 tablespoons drippings

A few bits of veal
½ cup chopped celery or
¼ teaspoon celery seed
1 tablespoon minced carrot
1 tablespoon minced onion

Melt the drippings from the veal stock; add the vegetables and cook for a few minutes, then add the stock and bay leaf. Simmer for 25 minutes, replenishing the stock as needed, season to taste with salt, pepper and mace. Serve with the vegetables in it. The bits of veal may be omitted, if desired.

Legume and Vegetable Soup

¼ cup dry lima beans
2 tablespoons green
  split peas
1 cup chopped carrots
1 cup chopped cabbage
2 tablespoons chopped
  turnips
2 tablespoons okra
  (fresh or canned)

I small onion, chopped
¼ cup chopped parsley
2 quarts water
¼ cup unroasted peanut
  butter or very finely
  chopped raw peanuts
I tablespoon salt

Wash the beans and peas and cook in water. Prepare the vegetables (except parsley) and combine with the peas and beans. Boil slowly 5 hours. At the end of the fourth hour of cooking add the chopped peanuts or peanut butter thinned with hot water. After another hour of cooking add salt, chopped parsley and boiling water to replenish what has boiled away. Serve with croutons.

Turkey Soup

I turkey carcass
water to cover
I small onion
I stick celery

½ teaspoon extract of
  beef
2 tablespoons rice
salt and season to taste

Break the carcass in pieces and remove all the stuffing; add water to cover and simmer 2 hours with the celery and onion. Remove the bones, strain and add the extract of beef and rice (after cooking in boiling salted water). Let the soup reach a boiling point, season and serve with croutons.

Brown Soup Stock

5 pounds skin or shank
of beef
4 quarts water
1 teaspoon peppercorn
5 cloves
½ bay leaf
1 sprig each summer savory
and marjoram, if available

½ teaspoon celery seed
or 2 stalks minced
celery
1/3 cups diced carrots
1/3 cups sliced onion
1/3 cups diced turnip
1 tablespoon salt
2 tablespoons beef
drippings

Cut meat from the bone and brown in the beef drippings. Crack the bone, add to the water with meat and bring slowly to boiling point. Simmer about 4 hours removing the scum as necessary and as fast as it rises. Then add the vegetables and seasonings and simmer 1 hour longer. Strain, cool, remove fat and clear as directed above.

Cream of Chicken Soup

4 cups chicken stock
2 cups milk
2 tablespoons flour
1 egg yolk (optional)
Few grains of mace

2 tablespoons butter or
margerine
2 tablespoons pearl or
1 tablespoon quick
cooking tapioca

Soak pearl tapioca over night, if used. Drain, put soup stock in a double boiler top and when hot add the tapioca (either kind) and cook until clear. Combine the mixtures, season with salt, pepper and mace and pour over the beaten egg yolk. Reheat for 2 minutes to cook the egg but not to a boiling point.

Cream of Celery Soup

4 cups celery leaves
    and tips
1 cup diced celery
4 cups white stock
1 cup light cream
2 egg yolks (optional)

1 slice onion
Bit of bay leaf
3½ tablespoons flour
2½ tablespoons butter
    or margerine
Sprig of parsley

Simmer the celery leaves, tips and seasonings in the white stock for 45 minutes. Cook the diced celery in 2 cups water until tender. Drain the celery adding the liquor to the stock. Thicken by melting butter and rubbing in the flour. Add the cream, strain, season to taste, add celery and reheat. Pour over beaten egg yolks, if used, and serve at once.

Split Pea Soup

½ cup split peas
2 quarts water
½ tablespoon sugar
1 pint milk
½ onion, minced

Few celery leaves
3 tablespoons fat or oil
3 tablespoons flour
Salt and pepper

Soak the peas over night in water to cover; drain, add to cold water with the sugar, onion and celery leaves. Cook slowly until peas are soft, add milk, thicken with the fat and flour mixture and rub through a sieve. Reheat, season and serve with buttered toast.

Cream of Oyster Soup

2 cups oysters	Salt and pepper
4 cups milk	1 cup whipped cream
1 tablespoon butter or	(unsweetened)
margerine	1 tablespoon flour

Chop the oysters, drain off the liquor and add to it an equal amount of water; heat slowly, skim well then add the chopped oysters and cook 3 minutes. Scald the milk. Melt the butter and work the flour and salt into it; add milk slowly mixing well together until smooth. Add oysters and seasoning. Add cream the last minute before serving.

Onion Soup

¼ cup diced carrot	1 cup rich milk or
1 stalk celery	light cream
8 tablespoons butter	1 egg yolk (optional)
1 tablespoon flour	Parmesan cheese
2 branches parsley	1 cup sliced onion
Toasted croutons	Salt and pepper
1½ meat stock	

Cook the carrot, celery, parsley and onion in butter until softened, then add the flour and stock and simmer for 20 minutes. Heat the cream, combine with egg yolk (if used), add to soup and cook for 2 minutes, stirring vigorously. Strain and serve with the croutons buttered lightly and sprinkle with Parmesan cheese.

Tomato Bisque

2 cups canned tomatoes
2 teaspoons sugar
¼ teaspoon soda
2 tablespoons butter or
bacon drippings

4 cups milk
1 slice onion
3 tablespoons flour
1 teaspoon salt
Dash pepper

Scald the milk with the onion. Cook the tomato with the sugar 15 minutes. Melt the fat, add flour and mix until smooth. Add milk gradually and heat but not to boiling point. Add the soda to the tomatoes, rub through a sieve, combine the mixtures, add the seasonings and serve without reheating.

Cream of Veal Soup

3 cups veal stock
(well seasoned)
1½ cups rich milk
2 tablespoons quick-
cooking tapioca

1 egg yolk (optional)
2 tablespoons flour
2 tablespoons butter
Salt and pepper

Add tapioca to the well seasoned veal stock and cook until clear. Prepare a sauce of butter, flour and milk, add to soup, season to taste and pour over egg yolk, slightly beaten, if used. Return to heat and stir for 2 minutes but not to boiling point.

Cream of Carrot Soup

1½ cups sliced carrots
1 sliced onion
Few sprigs parsley
3 cups water
1 tablespoon butter

1 14 oz. can evaporated milk
1 tablespoon flour
Salt, pepper and mace

Cook carrots, onions, parsley and water until tender, (if leftover carrots are used, cook only a few minutes). Rub carrots through a sieve, add milk and heat almost near a boiling point. Thicken with butter and flour (blended separately). Season with salt, pepper and a few grains of mace.

Barley and Tomato Soup

1½ cups tomato
1½ cups water
1 small onion, sliced
1 teaspoon salt

2 tablespoons pearl barley
½ tablespoon oil or margerine

Cook together all the ingredients except the barley for 20 minutes. Rub through a fine colander. Add water, if necessary, to make ¾ of a quart. Pour into a double boiler. Add the barley which has been thoroughly mashed and cook 4 or 5 hours.

Cream of Onion Soup

6 onions
2 tablespoons butter
3 cups water
1 tablespoon flour
1 tablespoon butter

2 cups scalded milk
1 egg yolk (beaten)
1 teaspoon salt
¼ teaspoon pepper
Parmesan cheese

Cut onions in fine pieces and saute in the butter until soft, but not brown; add water and let simmer for 20 minutes, then press through a sieve. Melt one tablespoon butter and blend in the flour, add scalded milk a little at a time and cook 5 minutes. Stir the thickened mixture into onion broth. When all is combined add the beaten egg yolk, salt and pepper. Serve piping hot with grated Parmesan cheese over top.

Cream of Corn and Mushroom Soup

2 tablespoons butter
½ cup shoepeg corn
with liquor
1½ cups water

1 can condensed cream
of mushroom soup
2 tablespoons chopped
pimento

Melt the butter in a saucepan, add corn with liquor and saute in butter 5 to 8 minutes. Add the cream of mushroom soup and stir well until corn is thoroughly mixed with the soup. Add water, heat and add chopped pimento for garnish.

Potato Vegetable Chowder

2 cups cubed raw potatoes
½ cup diced celery
¼ cup chopped onions
4 cups water
1 teaspoon salt

1/8 teaspoon red pepper
3 tablespoons flour
3 tablespoons butter
2 cups milk

Boil gently for 15 minutes in a covered pan the potatoes, celery, onions, water, salt and pepper. Blend flour and butter with milk. Simmer several minutes. Serves four.

Old-Fashioned Corn-Clam Chowder

1 can (1 lb., 1 oz.)
  cream-style corn
1 tablespoon butter
3 tablespoons chopped
  green pepper
1 tablespoon chopped onion
2 teaspoons flour

1 teaspoon salt
1/8 teaspoon pepper
2 cups milk
1 can (7½ oz.) Snow's
  minced Clams, drained
Whipped cream

In medium saucepan, bring corn and 1½ cups water to boiling. Reduce heat; simmer, uncovered, 20 minutes. In hot butter, in small skillet, saute pepper and onion 5 minutes. Remove skillet from heat. Blend in flour, salt and pepper until smooth. Gradually add ¼ cup milk. Stir into corn mixture; bring to boiling, stirring. Add rest of milk and clams; reheat gently. Serve hot, topped with whipped cream. Makes 4 to 6 servings.

Courtesy Borden Inc. — Foods Division
Snow Food Products

Corn and Tomato Chowder

1/3 cup butter
¼ cup chopped onions
½ cup sliced celery
2 cups diced potatoes
2 cups water

I can cream-style corn
2 cups milk
I can thick tomato soup
1½ teaspoon salt
Dash of pepper

Melt butter in a deep kettle, add onion and celery and cook until soft; add potatoes and 2 cups boiling water and cook until tender. Add corn and milk, heat near boiling point. Add soup, salt and pepper. Reheat before serving. Makes 6 to 8 servings.

Tuna Chowder

¼ cup diced salt pork
2 cups water
1/3 cup diced carrots
I diced large onion
1/3 cup chopped green pepper
1/3 cup chopped celery

2 cups diced potatoes
1/8 teaspoon pepper
¼ teaspoon salt
1 6½ oz. can tuna
I quart milk
2 tablespoons flour
½ cup water

Saute pork in kettle until golden brown. Add 2 cups water, carrots, onion, peppers, celery, potatoes, salt and pepper. Cook until all vegetables are tender and water boiled away. Add tuna and milk. Thicken with paste made from flour and water. Add enough paste to make consistency preferred. Serves 6.

Courtesy Boone's Custom House Wharf

Fish Chowder for Six

1-inch cube salt pork	4-6 medium potatoes
2 medium onions	1 pound fresh cusk
1 medium carrot	1 pint to 1 quart milk
1/16 pound butter	Salt and pepper

Start the pork at a very low temperature after having diced it very fine. While pork is cooking, slice the onions into 4-quart kettle. Then add the pork while hot, braising the onions slightly. Then add the carrot finely shredded and let all cook together for 15 minutes. Add cusk and potatoes all at once, having sliced all of the potatoes but one, saving it to be grated. Grated potato thickens chowder slightly, giving it body. Ample servings for 6.

Courtesy Boone's Custom House Wharf

Shrimp Chowder

3 medium onions, sliced	1 pound fresh shrimp
3 tablespoons fat	1 quart milk, heated
1 cup boiling water	1 cup (¼ lb.) grated
5 medium potatoes	American cheddar cheese
2 teaspoons salt	2 tablespoons minced
¼ teaspoon pepper	parsley

Saute onions in hot fat in deep kettle until tender. Add boiling water, then sliced potatoes, salt and pepper. Simmer, covered, 15 minutes, or until potatoes are tender. Then add shrimp, cooked and with viscera removed, the hot milk, in which the cheese has been melted, and parsley. Serve at once. Serves 4.

Courtesy Boone's Custom House Wharf

THE COAST OF MAINE

The ramifications of Maine's sea coast, it's extent and variety make it unique in America. It ranges from gently graded beaches to the bold, features of Mt. Desert. The coast of Maine contains every feature that the heart of man could desire. It abounds in more harbors, perhaps than the rest of America together, possesses. The tremendous surge of the tides, unequaled energy of the rivers have been harnessed for electrical power.

The Maine Coast is not merely grand, as are the cliffs of Grand Menan and the long beaches of Old Orchard. In its hidden waterways are numerous quiet stretches of water protected by fertile islands. On this coast pour out the fine fresh waters of Maine, the Kennebec, Androscoggin and Penobscot. For these rivers will bring one into a world of splendid beauty. Here the green of spring, the fullness of summer and flush of autumn spread themselves to the very margin of the streams.

Thus the seasons, the sun, the wind, the contour of the coastline with its varying elevations all assemble themselves to supply Maine with a natural drama. They answer to every mood in human experience, appealing to the gentle, the dreamy, the perceptive and the tragic. This is Maine and her coast.

Lobster Salad

3 large lobsters
2 hard-boiled eggs

1 head of lettuce
Salt

Cut lobster, eggs and lettuce into small pieces and mix with the following dressing. Save enough lettuce for garnish.

Salad Dressing

Mix together 1 teaspoon mustard, 1 teaspoon sugar, ½ teaspoon salt, yolks of 2 eggs; then drop in slowly; cup of butter melted and ½ cup vinegar very slowly; then add the beaten whites of 2 eggs, put into a double boiler and cook until thick. When very cold add 1 cup of cream well whipped.

Courtesy Boone's Custom House Wharf

Cranberry Salad

1 package lemon jello
1 cup hot water
1 cup sugar
1 orange (ground)

2 cups cranberries
    (ground)
1 apple (ground)

Place in small custard cups and when jelled place on lettuce and serve with any dressing.

Courtesy Boone's Custom House Wharf

Whiting Salad

2 cups flaked, cooked whiting
½ cup chopped celery
½ cup cooked frozen peas
2 tablespoons chopped sweet pickle
2 tablespoons chopped onion

3 hard cooked eggs, chopped
1 teaspoon salt
½ cup mayonnaise
2 tablespoons lemon juice
lettuce

Combine all ingredients except lettuce. Mix, using 2 silver forks, lifting so fish will not be broken into too small pieces. Serve on lettuce and garnish with cherry tomatoes and capers.

Note: Capers, delightful little pickled buds of Mediterranean shrub, are good in any salad but especially with fish giving it an effective garnish and pleasant taste treat.

Sailors' Salad

1 cup cooked carrot strips
1 cup cooked potato cubes
1 cup cooked string beans
2 hard cooked egg yolks

Shredded lettuce
French dressing
Chopped green pepper
Cottage cheese balls

Lay lettuce on plates. Mix potatoes and peppers with dressing. Add to lettuce, in flat patty shape. Arrange carrot strips like flower petals. Put balls of cottage cheese between. Sprinkle grated yolks of 2 hard-boiled eggs in center like flower centers. Serve slightly chilled, with extra dressing on side, and sweet mixed pickles.

Courtesy Boone's Custom House Wharf

Down East Shrimp Salad

Cook 1 pound fresh shrimp in boiling salted water with 1 bay leaf and 2 teaspoons vinegar for 10-15 minutes. Drain, wash in cold water, remove shells and remove black line that runs down back. Combine whole shrimp with ¾ cup bite-size chunks of lettuce, ½ cup sliced celery and ½ cup small stuffed olives. Toss lightly to distribute ingredients evenly. Serve ice cold. Season mayonnaise with salt, pepper, lemon juice and paprika to taste and serve in separate bowl. Do not mix into salad before serving, for best results.

Courtesy Boone's Custom House Wharf

Maine Sardine Cole Slaw

3 cans (3¾ or 4 oz. ea.) Maine sardines
4 cups shredded cabbage
¼ cup chopped onion
¼ cup chopped parsley
2 hard-cooked eggs, chopped
Cole Slaw Dressing
Salad greens
Paprika

Drain sardines and cut into large pieces. Combine cabbage, onion, parsley, eggs and dressing (see section on Salad Dressings). Arrange on salad greens. Top with sardines and sprinkle with paprika. Makes 6 servings.

Swordfish Salad Mold

1 cup flaked swordfish	2 tablespoons butter
1½ tablespoons flour	1 tablespoon gelatin
2 teaspoons mustard	¼ cup cold water
2 teaspoons sugar	¼ teaspoon celery salt
½ teaspoon salt	½ cup evaporated milk
1 egg	½ cup heavy cream
5 tablespoons lemon juice	(whipped)

Mix flour, water, sugar and salt in double boiler. Add egg, slightly beaten, evaporated milk and lemon juice. Stir over hot water until it thickens. Add butter, gelatin (which has been softened in cold water for 5 minutes) and celery salt. Mix well, then add swordfish (fish may be either freshly boiled or leftover fish). Cool, then add cream. Turn into a fish-shaped mold and chill. Serve on crisp lettuce, garnished with olives and strips of pimiento. Sliced tomatoes and cucumbers, butter rolls and fruit cup complete an appetizing dinner.

Courtesy Boone's Custom House Wharf

Hot Crabmeat Salad

½ pound shrimp	1 tablespoon diced green pepper
1 pound crabmeat	1 cup diced celery
1 tablespoon diced onion	1 cup mayonnaise for each cup of fish
Dash Worcestershire sauce	

Put in individual remekins or in large casserole. Cover with rolled corn flakes and melted butter. Bake 15 minutes about 375° or 400°.

Courtesy Boone's Custom House Wharf

Macaroni and Ham Salad

1½ cups elbow macaroni	15 stuffed olives, sliced
¾ cup minced ham	Mayonnaise or boiled
1¼ cups diced celery	dressing
1 teaspoon onion juice	Lettuce or cress

Boil the macaroni until tender, then cool. Combine with remaining ingredients, chill and serve on a bed of lettuce or cress. Garnish with whole olives.

Poinsettia Salad

2 No. 2 cans whole	Pimientoes
string beans	French dressing
1 head lettuce	Mayonnaise

Drain the beans and moisten well with the French dressing and let stand 1 hour in cold place. Shred the lettuce and make nests of it on individual plates. Dispose a mound of beans on it and arrange a poinsettia flower on the top of each serving cut from a pimiento. Form the center of the flower with mayonnaise.

Lenten Salad

2 cups shredded celery
½ cup radishes, sliced
½ cup broken walnut
    meat
Radish roses

2 hard-cooked eggs
Boiled or mayonnaise
    dressing
Lettuce

Shred the eggs; mix together other ingredients, add the dressing and then the egg. Mix lightly, dispose on lettuce nests and garnish with additional dressing and radish roses.

Kidney Bean Salad

2 cups cooked kidney
    beans
1 tablespoon vinegar
3 tablespoons olive oil
½ teaspoon salt
Lettuce or cress

2 tablespoons minced
    green pepper
1 tablespoon minced
    chives
1 tablespoon minced
    parsley

Mix the ingredients thoroughly; let stand 25 minutes to marinate, then arrange on lettuce. Garnish with green peppers stuffed with cabbage salad, parsley and pimiento strips.

Milady's Salad

6 slices tomato
¾ cup diced canned pineapple
¾ cup diced celery

Mayonnaise
Powdered parsley
Lettuce

Place slice of tomato on a nest of lettuce leaves. Combine the pineapple and celery with a little mayonnaise and put spoonful of this mixture on each slice of tomato. Top with extra mayonnaise, sprinkle with parsley and serve very cold.

Cocoanut Salad

½ cocoanut, grated
2 apples, pared, cored and chopped
1 cup celery, chopped
3 Chile peppers

2 tablespoons onions, chopped
1 tablespoon parsley, coarsely chopped

Mix ingredients; cover with 2 measures of French dressing, chill and serve in lettuce shells or in scooped-out tomatoes.

Tomato and Lima Bean Salad

4 tomatoes	½ cup nut meats, finely
1½ cups cooked lima beans	chopped
1 tablespoon parsley	2 tablespoons minced
1 small onion, grated	celery or dash celery
Salt and pepper to taste	salt

Cut off top of each tomato and remove the pulp. Add the onion, parsley, nuts, celery and seasoning to the beans. Mix above ingredients with little French dressing and fill tomatoes with the mixture. Pour more dressing over the top and serve separately.

Fruit and Nut Salad

1 large pineapple	1 dozen Maraschino
¼ pound shelled almonds	cherries
¼ pound shelled bilberts	Cream or mayonnaise
Lettuce	dressing

Remove rind and eyes from the pineapple and cut the flesh into small pieces, leaving out the hard core. Blanch the nuts by pouring boiling water over them and allow to stand a few minutes until the skins can be easily removed. Chop finely and add to the pineapple. Pile in little heaps on lettuce leaves, cover with the dressing and decorate with cherries.

TWO LIGHTS AND PORTLAND HEAD

In 1829 two stone lighthouses were completed in a section near the "pitch" of Cape Elizabeth. The twin towers, known as Two Lights, draw many visitors to the Cape's endlessly breaking surface of unique rock formations each year. A colorful history of construction and reconstruction of these towers has been enjoyed by natives and tourists alike over the years. A navigator could tell his exact position from the position of the two lighthouses.

The stone lighthouses were replaced by two towers of cast iron in 1873. They stood 300 feet apart with one beacon flashing and the other fixed. These beams continued to guide seamen for half a century. The Western light was discontinued in 1924. The remaining tower was converted to electricity and today has become the most brilliant beacon on the eastern coast.

Just down the coast from Two Lights is Portland Head Light on Cape Elizabeth. This single lighthouse is one of the oldest in the country, and certainly the first in Maine. The original tower, built of rubble-stone, was the first erected in the new government under George Washington. And, it is that fieldstone lighthouse that still stands, with modern day electricity replacing the whale oil and kerosene power of old.

Maine Potato Salad

2½ cups small cooked
   potato cubes
1 cucumber, pared and
   sliced
1 cup diced celery
1 pimiento, chopped

2 hard-cooked eggs
Boiled salad dressing
Oil and vinegar or
   lemon juice
Lettuce
Salt and herb seasoning

Mix the cubed potato, cucumber, diced celery, pimiento and eggs together in a bowl. Pour over the oil and vinegar the amount desired. Toss lightly but mix thoroughly the boiled salad dressing and salt and herbs. Keep very cold until served.

Peanut and Potato Salad

3 cups diced cooked
   potatoes
3 hard-cooked eggs
2 cups diced celery
1 cup shredded cabbage

1 cup peanut meats
Parsley
Lettuce
French dressing
Boiled dressing

Marinate the potato and celery in the French dressing, then mix half the peanut meats, chopped and a tablespoon of minced parsley with potato. Add ½ teaspoon of onion juice, if desired. Blend with the boiled dressing and arrange on lettuce leaves. Garnish with parsley, egg and remaining nut meats.

Shamrock Salad

2 large green peppers
1 large package cream cheese
¼ cup chopped walnut meats
Lettuce

French or mayonnaise dressing
2 tablespoons stuffed olives
2 tablespoons cream
Salt and pepper

Remove the stem ends from the peppers and scrape out the seeds and cores. Let peppers stand in cold, salted water for 2 hours, then drain and pack full of the cheese, nuts and olives creamed together and season to taste and moistened with cream. Let stand to become very firm, then slice across in ¼-inch pieces; pour over a little French dressing and serve two slices to each on a nest of lettuce hearts. Garnish with radish roses and mayonnaise.

Spring Salad

¾ cup sliced scullions
1 cup cooked diced carrots
1 bunch watercress

1½ cups sliced, cooked new beets
5 tablespoons French dressing

Dredge the scullions with salt and pepper and pour over 2 tablespoons vinegar. Add ½ tablespoon sugar. Let stand 1 hour in a cold place. Combine the carrots and beets with the French dressing and add the scullions, drained. Let stand 15 minutes; drain, toss the cress in the dressing and mix in salad.

Brown Rice Salad

2 cups boiled brown rice
1 cup diced celery
1 minced green pepper
½ tablespoon grated onion
3 tablespoons olive oil

1 tablespoon vinegar or
 lemon juice
½ teaspoon salt and herbs
Tomato catsup
Lettuce or cress

Mix together the salad ingredients and arrange on the lettuce. Pour over a little catsup and garnish further with parsley, if desired.

Harlequin Salad

1 cup red cabbage
1 cup white cabbage
1 cup French peas
½ cup beets

1 diced onion
½ cup diced carrot
Salt and pepper to
 taste

Cook peas, beets and carrot until tender. Shave the cabbage, cut and dice onion into small pieces and mix with vegetables. Pour French dressing over the salad 1 hour before serving and again at time of serving.

Dandelion and Bacon Salad

1 quart young dandelions   1½ tablespoon vinegar
3 bacon strips, cubed   Few grains cayenne

Clean the greens thoroughly being careful to leave their shape. Plunge into boiling water, then at once into cold water. Let stand 20 minutes. Meanwhile, fry the bacon and to 3 tablespoons of hot fat add the vinegar and cayenne. Drain the dandelions, mix well with this dressing and garnish with the bacon.

Elite Fruit Salad

2 lettuce hearts
2 bananas, sliced
1 cup Malaga grapes
    (halved and seeded)
2 tart apples, diced

½ cup pecan nuts, chopped
    coarse
Mayonnaise or honey
    dressing

Shred the lettuce into pieces. Peel and halve the grapes, removing the seeds; pare and cut apples into small cubes. Combine and marinate 30 minutes in a dressing made of 2 tablespoons olive oil and 1 tablespoon lemon juice. Add the nuts and bananas, drain and garnish on individual plates with tine lettuce leaves with a spoon of dressing on each serving.

Date and Apple Salad

1 cup stoned and quartered dates
2 cups diced tart apple pulp
½ cup English or black walnuts
Lettuce

Few grains salt
1½ tablespoons lemon juice
3 tablespoons olive oil
1 tablespoon powdered sugar

Mix together the oil, lemon juice, sugar and salt thoroughly. Pour over the dates and apples separately. Let stand 30 minutes in cold place to season, then toss together, arrange on lettuce leaves and sprinkle with the nuts (chopped).

Cherry and Nut Salad

½ can or 1 pint fresh cherries
Lettuce

Shelled peanuts
Mayonnaise or boiled oil dressing

Stone the cherries and replace the pits with the nuts. Arrange on lettuce leaves and serve with the desired dressing.

Prune and Tangerine Salad

30 sections of tangerine
   oranges
18 prunes
Orange juice
Lettuce

Walnut meats
French fruit salad
   dressing
Parsley or celery tips

Soak the prunes for 2 hours in orange juice; then remove the stones, replacing with walnut meats. Pour French dressing over the orange sections and let stand for 30 minutes. Drain; arrange individually on salad plates and pile the prunes in the center. Pour over the drained French dressing and garnish with desired salad green.

Porcupine Salad

6 whole canned pears
1 cup browned and
   shredded almonds
12 large whole cloves
4 tablespoons olive oil

1 tablespoon lemon juice
2 tablespoons grapefruit
   juice
Few grains salt
Lettuce

Drain the pears and stick in two cloves at the small end to represent eyes. Place the pears in a dish and marinate in a French dressing made of olive oil, lemon juice and grapefruit juice with seasonings. After 30 minutes stick the shredded almonds in each pear to represent quills and serve on lettuce.

Cole Slaw Dressing

½ cup salad oil
3 tablespoons vinegar
1 tablespoon chopped
  green pepper
1 tablespoon chopped
  pimiento

1 tablespoon chopped
  sweet pickle
1 teaspoon salt
¼ teaspoon paprika
Dash cayenne pepper

Combine all ingredients and mix thoroughly. Makes approximately ¾ cup dressing.

Curry Dressing

½ tablespoon salt
¾ teaspoon mustard
2 tablespoons sugar
Few grains cayenne
6 tablespoons weak
  vinegar

1 tablespoon flour
3 egg yolks
2 tablespoons melted
  butter or oil
½ teaspoon curry powder
1¼ cups milk

Mix the dry ingredients, add the egg yolks, slightly beaten, the butter and milk; then pour in the vinegar slowly and cook over boiling water until the mixture thickens, stirring constantly. Strain and cool.

Peanut Butter Salad Dressing

2 tablespoons peanut
butter
1 tablespoon olive oil
Dash of paprika

1 tablespoon tarragon
vinegar
½ tablespoon lemon juice
1 cup any boiled dressing

Combine above ingredients and beat thoroughly. Serve with fruit salad.

Sweet or Sour Cream Dressing

2 egg yolks or 1 egg
½ teaspoon salt
Few grains cayenne
4 tablespoons tarragon
vinegar

¼ teaspoon mustard
1 tablespoon sugar
2 tablespoons butter
¾ cup whipped cream
(sweet or sour)

Mix together egg yolks and dry ingredients in a double boiler top. Add vinegar and cook over hot water until thickened, then add the butter, bit by bit. Cool mixture; fold in whipped cream just before serving. For fruit salads.

Cream Honey Salad Dressing

4 egg yolks
½ cup honey
Juice of 1 lemon
1/3 teaspoon salt

1 cup slightly sour or
  sweet cream
1/3 cup olive oil
¼ teaspoon paprika

Beat the egg yolks thoroughly, then pour in the honey, which should be boiling hot. Cook for a moment, beating continuously, then fold in the oil, lemon juice and the cream, beaten stiff. For fruit salad.

French Dressing

3 tablespoons olive oil
1 tablespoon vinegar
1/3 teaspoon salt

Few grains paprika
Few grains pepper

Combine ingredients and beat thoroughly.

French Fruit Salad Dressing
3 tablespoons olive oil
1 tablespoon lemon juice
1/8 teaspoon salt
½ tablespoon powdered sugar

Combine ingredients and beat thoroughly.

Rich Salad Dressing — Cooked
½ tablespoon mustard
½ tablespoon salt
1 tablespoon sugar
1 tablespoon onion juice (optional)
1 cup milk
1 cup mild vinegar
1 tablespoon corn starch
3 eggs or 6 egg yolks

Mix the ingredients together, add the eggs and onion juice and beat well. Stir in the milk, and cook over hot water until thick, then add the vinegar, slowly, beating thoroughly. Strain and cool.

Cooked Olive Oil Dressing

2 tablespoons olive oil	1 cup olive oil
2 tablespoons flour	1 teaspoon salt
2 tablespoons lemon juice	¼ teaspoon cayenne pepper
Boiling water	¼ teaspoon mustard
1 egg yolk, beaten	1 egg white

Blend the 2 tablespoons olive oil, flour and lemon juice in a measuring cup. Fill the cup with boiling water, transfer to a double boiler and cook until thickened, stirring constantly. Pour over egg yolk, beating constantly and cool. Add oil and seasonings gradually, then thin the mixture with the egg white, whipped stiff.

Maple Sirup Dressing

1 egg	Juice of ½ lemon
1 cup maple sirup	

Beat egg slightly with a fork, add sirup and lemon juice, and cook in double boiler over hot water until thick, stirring constantly. Chill, Add 2 tablespoons or more, according to taste, to 1 cup whipped cream. For fruit salads.

EGGS

AND

OMELETS

Soft-Cooked Eggs

Cold Water Method: Cover eggs in pan with water to come at least 1 inch above the eggs. Bring rapidly to boiling. Turn off heat and if necessary set pan off burner to prevent further boiling. Cover and let stand 2-4 minutes depending on individual taste. Cool eggs promptly in cold water for several seconds to prevent further cooking and to make them easy to handle.

Boiling Water Method: Bring water in pan to rapid boiling, using enough to cover eggs as above. To avoid cracked shells, place cold eggs in warm water. Transfer eggs to water with spoon, turn off heat, and if necessary, set pan off burner to prevent further boiling. Cover and let stand 6-8 minutes. Cool as above.

Hard-Cooked Eggs

Cold Water Method: Follow directions for Soft-Cooked Eggs— Cold Water Method. Let stand 15 minutes. Cool promptly and thoroughly in cold water — this makes the shells easier to remove and helps prevent dark surface on yolks.

Boiling Water Method: Follow directions for Soft-Cooked Eggs — Boiling Water Method, but reduce heat to keep water below simmering and hold 20 minutes. Cool as above.

Fried Eggs

Method 1: Heat 1 to 2 tablespoons fat in a skillet just hot enough to sizzle a drop of water. Break and slip eggs into skillet — from a sauce dish if preferred. Reduce heat immediately. Cook slowly to desired doneness, 3-4 minutes. Baste with fat during cooking. Instead of basting, skillet may be covered or eggs may be turned over.

Method 2: Use just enough fat to grease skillet. Proceed as above. Cook over low heat until edges turn white, about 1 minute. Add ½ teaspoon water for one egg, decreasing proportion slightly for each additional egg. Cover skillet tightly to hold in steam which bastes the egg. Cook to desired doneness.

Broiled Eggs

Heat just enough fat to grease a shallow skillet or flame-proof baking dish. When fat is just hot enough to sizzle a drop of water, break eggs and slip into skillet — from a sauce dish if preferred. Cook on top the range just until edges turn white, about 1 minute. Place skillet in heated broiler and broil eggs at moderate temperature to desired doneness, 2-4 minutes.

Variations: (1) Pour 1 tablespoon of cream per egg into skillet when edges are white and before placing in broiler. (2) Sprinkle over eggs 1 teaspoon grated cheese or buttered crumbs before placing in broiler.

Baked (Shirred) Eggs

Break and slip 1 or 2 eggs into greased individual shallow baking dishes. Bake in slow oven (325 F.), 12-18 minutes, depending upon firmness desired. Serve from baking dishes.

Variations: (1) Circle a strip of partially cooked bacon around edge of dish. Line bottom of dishes with buttered crumbs. (2) Line bottom of dishes with buttered crumbs. Place a slice of cheese atop crumbs, then break eggs into dish. Top with grated cheese or crumbs. Proceed as above.

Scrambled Eggs

4 eggs	1/8 teaspoon pepper
4 tablespoons milk or cream	1 tablespoon butter, margarine or oil
½ teaspoon salt, scant	

Mix eggs, milk, salt and pepper with fork or spoon — mixing thoroughly if a uniform yellow is preferred or mixing slightly if steaks of white and yellow are preferred. Heat fat in skillet (approximately 8-inch) just hot enough to sizzle drop of water. Pour in egg mixture. Reduce heat enough to cook egg quickly, lifting from the bottom and sides as the mixture thickens. As the cooked mixture is lifted, the thin, uncooked part should flow to the bottom. Avoid constand stirring. Cook until eggs are thickened throughout but still moist, about 5-8 minutes. 2 servings.

Poached Eggs

Bring water in shallow pan to the boiling point — enough to have about 2 inches of water. Reduce heat to hold temperature at simmering. Break each egg into a sauce dish and slip egg into water quickly at the surface. Cook 3-5 minutes depending on the firmness desired. Remove eggs with slotted pancake turner or spoon, and drain.

Creamed Egg Ramekins

½ cup sliced celery
¼ cup chopped onion
2 tablespoons butter
1 can (10 oz.) frozen condensed cream of shrimp soup
1/3 cup milk
4 slices hot toast

¼ cup sour cream
4 hard-cooked eggs, quartered
3 tablespoons soft butter
1 teaspoon garlic salt (optional)
Parsley

In saucepan, cook celery and onion in butter until tender; add soup and milk. Heat, stirring occasionally. Blend in sour cream; add eggs and heat through. Combine butter with garlic salt if desired, and spread on toast. Serve creamed eggs over toast in individual ramekins. Garnish with parsley. Makes 4 servings.

Barbecued Omelet

2 eggs, slightly beaten
2 tablespoons water
4 drops liquid smoke
4 drops Tabasco

2 drops garlic juice
¼ teaspoon salt
1 tablespoon butter

Mix eggs, water, liquid smoke, tabasco, garlic juice and salt with fork. Heat butter in omelet pan (8-inch) just hot enough to sizzle a drop of water. Pour 1 dipper of egg mixture into pan. Eggs will set at edges immediately. Cook over moderately high temperature, shaking pan rapidly back and forth or in circular motion. With spatula or fork draw cooked portions at edges toward center so that uncooked portions flow to bottom. Keep omelet relatively flat. When eggs are set and surface is still moist, fold or roll omelet and slide onto serving plate. Cooking time 1½ minutes or less. Recipe for 1 serving.

Fruit Omelet

Prepare favorite omelet and serve with sliced or diced fresh fruit. Or thicken canned fruit such as cherries, peaches or pineapples and serve hot over omelet. Also try applesauce, pears, plums, apricots, raspberries or oranges.

French or Plain Omelet

3 eggs	1/8 teaspoon pepper
3 tablespoons water	1 tablespoon butter,
3/8 teaspoon salt	margarine or oil

Mix eggs, water, salt and pepper with a fork until yolks and whites are blended. Meanwhile, heat butter, margarine or oil in an omelet pan or heavy skillet just hot enough to sizzle a drop of water. Pour in egg mixture all at once. Mixture should begin to cook immediately at the outer edges. With the fork, lift cooked portions at edges so uncooked portions flow underneath. Slide pan rapidly back and forth over the heat to keep mixture in motion and sliding freely to avoid sticking. When mixture is set, the egg no longer flows freely. The omelet is moist and creamy on top. Let it cook about 1 minute to brown the bottom slightly. Fold or roll, and serve promptly on a warm platter. Makes 1 or 2 servings.

Herb Omelet

Add one teaspoon fresh snipped herbs or ¼ teaspoon dry herbs to ingredients of French Omelet before cooking. Try: basil, celery seed, chives, dill, marjoram, mint, onion or parsley.

Puffy Omelet

4 eggs, separated	1/8 teaspoon pepper
½ teaspoon salt	1 tablespoon butter,
¼ cup water	margarine or oil

Add salt and water to egg whites. Beat until stiff and shiny and whites leave peaks when beater is withdrawn. Add pepper to yolks and beat until thick and lemon-colored. Fold yolks into egg whites. Meanwhile heat butter, margarine or oil in large skillet with heat-proof handle (10-inch diameter) until just hot enough to sizzle a drop of water. Pour in omelet mixture. Reduce heat. Level surface gently. Cook slowly until puffy and lightly browned on bottom, about 5 minutes. Lift omelet gently at edge to judge color. Place in a slow oven (325 F). Bake until knife inserted into center comes out clean, 12-15 minutes. To serve: Tear gently, using 2 forks, into pie-shaped pieces. Invert "wedges" on serving plate so that browned bottom comes to top. Or, omelet may be folded in half. Makes 2-3 servings.

10-Minute Omelet

4 eggs, separated	1 tablespoon soft butter
¼ teaspoon salt	or margarine
1/8 teaspoon pepper	1 tablespoon water
1 tablespoon flour	

Beat egg whites with salt until stiff but not dry. Beat egg yolks with pepper, flour, butter or margarine and water until fluffy. Fold beaten yolks into beaten whites. Pour into well-greased 8 or 9-inch skillet heated until a drop of water sizzles. Cover tightly. Reduce heat to low and cook 8-10 minutes on top of range until surface of omelet is "dry" when touched lightly with fingertip. Fold in half and serve promptly. Makes 2 to 3 servings.

Spanish Omelet

Prepare Puffy or 10-Minute Omelet and serve with following Spanish Sauce:

1 tablespoon butter, margarine or oil

2 tablespoons minced onion

2 tablespoons minced green pepper

1/8 teaspoon cayenne pepper

3 cans (8 oz.) tomato sauce

1 tablespoon sugar

1 tablespoon Worcestershire

Cook onion and green pepper in butter over low heat several minutes. Do not brown. Add tomato sauce and seasonings; simmer 20 minutes or until sauce is thickened. Makes sufficient sauce for 2 Puffy or 10-Minute Omelets.

Noodle Omelet

4 oz. (1½ cups) noodles

2 tablespoons chopped onion

3 tablespoons butter, margarine or oil

3 eggs

2 tablespoons water

½ teaspoon salt

1/8 teaspoon pepper

Cook noodles according to package directions. Drain well. Cook onion in butter or margarine until soft but not brown. Add noodles and blend. Blend eggs, water, salt and pepper with fork. Mix well but do not beat frothy; pour over noodles in skillet. Cook rapidly, lifting mixture with fork, at the same time tipping skillet to let uncooked mixture flow to bottom of skillet. Keep mixture as level as possible. Shake skillet while cooking to be sure mixture is not sticking at any point. When mixture no longer flows, reduce heat for a minute to "set" the omelet and brown the bottom. Fold in half. Serve with crisp chicken livers, bacon, sausage or apple rings. 3-4 servings.

Poultry or Meat Omelet

Fold ½ cup diced or chopped, cooked chicken, turkey or duckling meat into omelet mixture before cooking. Or add meat to 1 can (10½ oz.) cheese or cream of mushroom soup. Serve over favorite omelet. Or try adding crisp crumbled bacon, cooked sausage, dried beef, smoked turkey, tuna fish or shrimp.

Mushroom-Cheese Omelet

1 tablespoon butter, margarine or oil	4 eggs, separated
	¼ teaspoon salt
¼ pound process American cheese, diced	¼ pound mushrooms, sliced
	2 tablespoons butter,
¼ cup milk	margarine or oil
1/8 teaspoon pepper	

While mixing omelet ingredients, heat 2 tablespoon butter or margarine in covered 10-inch electric skillet with temperature control set at 320 F. Heat cheese and milk in saucepan over low heat until cheese is melted and free of lumps, stirring constantly. Add pepper to yolks and beat until thick and lemon-colored. Gradually pour cheese sauce into yolks, stirring constantly. Add salt to whites and beat until stiff but not dry. Fold yolk mixture into whites, gently but thoroughly. Tip skillet to spread butter evenly over bottom; pour in omelet mixture, level surface gently and cover. Reduce heat to 240 F and cook until surface is "dry" (touch lightly with fingertip) and knife inserted in center comes out clean, about 20 minutes. Meanwhile cook sliced mushrooms in butter about 5 minutes and spoon over omelet. Fold and serve immediately. Makes 3-4 servings.

Seafood Omelet

FILLING:
1 package frozen peas
1 can (7¾ oz.) salmon
1 can cream of mushroom
  soup, undiluted
Salt and pepper to taste

OMELET:
9 eggs
½ cup water
1 teaspoon salt
Butter, margarine or
  oil for cooking

Combine filling ingredients in a saucepan and heat. Keep hot until omelets are baked. To prepare omelets: Beat eggs, water and salt together until light and foamy. Preheat griddle to 300-325 F (low heat), brushing entire surface with butter, margarine or oil. Slowly pour ½ cup of the egg mixture on the griddle for each omelet, allowing it to spread. When omelets are set and lightly browned on the bottom, place 2 tablespoons of filling in the center of each omelet. Fold both sides over with narrow spatula. Makes 12 omelets or 6 servings.

Creamed Eggs with Sardines

4 tablespoons butter
¼ cup soft, stale bread
  crumbs
1 cup thin cream or top
  milk

½ box sardines
2 hard-cooked eggs,
  finely chopped
½ teaspoon salt
¼ teaspoon paprika
1/8 teaspoon pepper

Melt butter, add bread crumbs and cream, and bring to boiling point. Add eggs, sardines freed from skin and bones, and seasonings. Bring to boiling point again and serve at once. Serves 2 or 3.

FISH

AND

SHELLFISH

Deviled Crabs

2 tablespoons butter
2 tablespoons flour
1 cup soup stock
2 egg yolks

1 cup chopped crabmeat
¼ cup sliced mushrooms
1 teaspoon parsley
Salt and pepper

Make a sauce of butter, flour and stock and add other ingredients, except parsley and cook several minutes. Add parsley. Wash and trim crab shells, fill rounding with mixture, and sprinkle with buttered crumbs. Crease on top with case knife, making 3 parallel lines and 3 short lines branching from outside parallel lines. Bake till crumbs are brown at 350°.

Jellied Tuna Fish

2 tablespoons gelatin
½ cup cold water
¼ cup mayonnaise
½ teaspoon salt
1/8 teaspoon paprika
1 tablespoon vinegar

1 cup tuna fish (flaked)
1 cup chopped celery
1 cup chopped olives
½ cup chopped green pepper
3 tablespoons chopped pimiento

Soak gelatin in cold water 5 minutes. Dissolve over hot water and add mayonnaise, salt, paprika, vinegar. Mix together flaked tuna, celery, olives, green pepper and pimiento, and add to mayonnaise mixture. Put into fancy mould which has been dipped in cold wa   and chill until firm. When ready to serve unmould on crisp lett e and garnish with mayonnaise.

Salmon Loaf

2 cups flaked salmon
1 cup bread crumbs
1 tablespoon chopped onion
2 eggs

1 tablespoon chopped parsley
1 teaspoon salt
Dash pepper

Put all ingredients into a bowl and mix thoroughly. Shape into loaf pan; add ½ cup water. Bake in moderate oven 350° for 35 minutes. Tuna, haddock, swordfish or halibut may be used instead of salmon.

Salmon Casserole

4 potatoes
4 slices bacon
1 cup peas (optional)
1 egg
¼ cup bread crumbs

1 minced onion
2 cups salmon
¾ cup milk
Dash salt
Pepper to taste

Put layer of peeled, sliced potatoes into buttered casserole then layer of salmon, peas, onion and bacon. Mix egg and milk and pour over salmon. Sprinkle with crumbs and bake in moderate oven 350° for 50-60 minutes.

Turban of Fish

2 pounds haddock	Grated rind I lemon
½ bay leaf	I teaspoon salt
Juice I lemon	I tablespoon butter
I cup water	¼ teaspoon celery salt
I½ cups soft bread crumbs	Cayenne
I½ cups scalded milk	Whites 2 eggs, beaten stiff
Yolks 2 eggs, beaten	

Cook fish with bay leaf, lemon juice and water. Remove and flake. Combine hot milk and bread crumbs (no crusts). Stir in beaten egg yolks, lemon rind and seasonings. Fold in stiffly beaten egg whites. Pour into loaf pan lined with oiled paper. Set into a pan containing ½ inch hot water and bake at 350° about 1 hour. Unmold on platter and garnish top with whole blanched salted almonds. Serve with white sauce to which chopped almonds have been added.

Baked Stuffed Haddock

I 4 pound haddock	2 cups Sweet Pickle
Salt and pepper	Stuffing
2 tablespoons butter	

Wipe fish with damp cloth. Clean and remove all bones possible. Season inside with salt and pepper. Put stuffing in and secure with toothpicks. Place in baking pan, add ½ cup water and brush top of fish with butter. Bake 1 hour at 350°, basting with butter occasionally.

For *Sweet Pickle Stuffing* combine 2 cups bread crumbs, 1 teaspoon grated onion, ½ cup chopped celery, ¼ cup chopped sweet pickles, ½ teaspoon salt and 3 tablespoons melted butter.

Baked Cream Haddock Fillets

2 pounds haddock fillets
¼ teaspoon salt
1/8 teaspoon pepper
1 can cream of celery soup

1 teaspoon prepared mustard
½ cup buttered crumbs
1 tablespoon minced parsley

Cut fillets in serving pieces and place in greased shallow pan. Sprinkle with seasonings. Heat celery soup and pour over fillets. Sprinkle with buttered crumbs and parsley. Bake 35 minutes at 350°. Serves 6.

Sweet and Sour Mackerel

2 large Maine mackerel
1 carrot
1 onion
2 sugar lumps

2 bay leaves
Salt and peppercorns
1 tablespoon vinegar

Clean mackerel removing heads and tails. Cut each fish into 4 pieces. Place in saucepan and cover with water. Cut carrot and onion and add to fish along with a little salt, the sugar, vinegar, bay leaves and 5-6 peppercorns. Bring to boiling, then simmer for 30 minutes. May be served hot or cold.

Pollock Fillets with Dressing

2 cups soft bread crumbs	2 tablespoons butter
¼ cup chopped onion	2 tablespoons flour
1 tablespoon chopped	1 cup water
parsley	Juice ½ lemon
Salt and pepper	6 pollock fillets
Water to moisten dressing	

Combine first four ingredients to make dressing, moistening with just enough water so you can mold to size and shape of fish fillets. Place dressing on heat-proof platter or utility dish and arrange fillets on dressing. Sprinkle fish with salt and pepper. Make sauce of remaining ingredients and pour around fish. Bake at 425° for 20 minutes.

Cusk Pie

1 pound cooked cusk	1 tablespoon minced
fish sticks	green pepper
½ teaspoon salt	1 cup frozen peas
¼ teaspoon pepper	1 can celery soup
2½ cups mashed potato	

Flake cooked fish and combine with other ingredients except potato. Place in well greased casserole and cover with hot, seasoned mashed potato. Bake just long enough to heat through (15-20 minutes) then turn on the broiler to brown potatoes.

Baked Halibut Steak with Cheese

1 slice halibut, 1-inch thick	½ cup fine bread crumbs
Butter	½ cup grated Parmesan
	Salt and paprika

Place slice of halibut in greased pan. Sprinkle with salt and paprika and dot with butter. Bake in 350° oven for 15 minutes. Combine bread crumbs and cheese and sprinkle over fish. Dot with butter. Bake another 15-20 minutes or until done.

Halibut-Lobster Casserole

3 cups cooked rice	¼ cup butter
2 cups flaked boiled halibut	1 tablespoon chopped onion
1 cup lobster meat	1 tablespoon chopped
1 can pimiento, sliced	green pepper
2 cups milk	¼ cup shredded cheese
1 cup cream	Salt and pepper
5 tablespoons flour	

Melt butter, blend in flour; add milk and cream and cook, stirring constantly until thickened. Saute onion and green pepper in a little butter and add to sauce. Mix remaining ingredients with sauce. Put into buttered baking dish and cover with buttered crumbs. Bake 30 minutes at 350°. Serves 8-10.

Whiting Dinner Casserole

2 tablespoons butter
1½ tablespoons flour
½ teaspoon salt
1/8 teaspoon pepper
1½ cups milk
2 teaspoons chopped
parsley

1 small can sliced
mushrooms
1 small onion, minced
2 tablespoons butter
1½ pounds whiting fillets
2 cups sliced raw potatoes

Make white sauce of 2 tablespoons butter, flour, milk and seasonings. Saute mushrooms and onions in other 2 tablespoons butter. Combine one cup of the sauce with cooked onion mixture and the fish which has been cut in one inch pieces. Place in greased baking dish, cover with sliced potatoes and rest of the sauce. Bake in 350° oven 60-70 minutes. Serves 6.

Hake Casserole

2 cups white sauce
1 cup cooked hake, flaked
1 cup frozen peas
Salt and pepper

1 tablespoon diced pimento
2 sliced hard boiled eggs
½ cup buttered crumbs
½ cup grated cheese

Put into casserole by layers, starting with white sauce. Top with buttered crumbs and grated cheese. Sprinkle top with seasoned salt. Bake 30 minutes at 350°.

Maine Whiting with Mushrooms

4-8 oz. Maine whiting
¾ cup milk
4 tablespoons flour
3 tablespoons butter
1 onion
½ pound mushrooms
3 tablespoons butter

Salt and pepper
Nutmeg
Juice 1 lemon
1 tablespoon chopped
   parsley
3 tablespoons butter

Clean and wash fish. Pat dry with paper towel. Pour milk into soup plate and spread flour on plate. Dip fish in milk, then in flour. Heat first 3 tablespoons butter in large skillet and saute whiting over medium heat, turning fish until well browned on both sides. Peel and chop onions very fine. Trim, wash and chop mushrooms. Heat second 3 tablespoons butter in small skillet, saute mushrooms and onion until mushrooms are almost dry. Season with salt and pepper and nutmeg. Place fish on heat-proof serving dish. Spread with mushroom mixture. Place in 400° oven for 1 minute. Heat the last 3 tablespoons butter until brown. Add juice of 1 lemon and pour over fish. Sprinkle with chopped parsley. Serves 4.

Baked Ocean Perch

1 lemon, sliced thin
1 onion, sliced thin
1½ pounds ocean perch
   fillets
Salt and pepper

1 cup soured cream
¼ teaspoon salt
¼ teaspoon paprika
1 teaspoon prepared
   mustard

Cover bottom of greased baking dish with lemon and onion slices. Sprinkle lightly with salt and pepper. Lay fillets on top. Cover. Bake 20 minutes in 400° oven. Remove cover. Combine sour cream and seasonings and spread over fish. Broil until brown. Serves 5.

Fillet of Sole Marguery

8 flounder fillets	3 tablespoons butter
Salt and paprika	3 tablespoons flour
1/3 cup white wine	Pepper
2½ cups fish stock	¼ cup grated Parmesan
1 boiled lobster	cheese
18 cooked Maine shrimp	

Place fillets in buttered baking dish. Sprinkle with salt and paprika; add wine. Cover with aluminum foil and bake 15 minutes at 350°. Combine fish stock, shell of lobster and 6 clams. Simmer until reduced to 1 cup. Blend butter and flour, add strained stock and ¼ cup liquid from fillets. On a heat-proof serving platter arrange fillets and pour strained sauce on top. Garnish with lobster meat and shrimps; sprinkle with cheese and bake in 350° oven until cheese is melted and fillets are hot. Serves 8.

Sardines with State O' Maine Sauce

1 can Maine sardines	1 tablespoon water
2 cloves garlic	2 tablespoons salad oil
1 tablespoon chopped onion	¼ teaspoon salt
1 tablespoon minced green	½ teaspoon celery salt
pepper	¼ teaspoon paprika
1 tablesoon prepared	½ teaspoon black pepper
mustard	¼ teaspoon red pepper
1 teaspoon grated	Juice of ½ lemon
horseradish	

Arrange sardines on platter. Place slices of lemon, tomato and pickle on platter as a border. Crush garlic in mixing bowl. Add onion and green pepper, crushing these with the garlic. Add mustard, horseradish (mixed with water) and salad oil. Mix thoroughly. Add remainder of seasonings. Blend well and pour over sardines. Serves 4.

New England Salt Fish Dinner

1½ -2 pounds salt cod
¼ pound salt pork
6 potatoes

12 small beets
6 onions
1½ cups white sauce

Cut fish in portions suitable for serving. Cover with cold water and allow to stand for 1 or 2 hours, changing the water several times. Drain, cover with fresh cold water and bring slowly to boiling point. Drain. Dice the salt pork and fry until brown. Cook vegetables separately. Arrange fish on hot platter and cover with white sauce. Garnish with pork and arrange vegetables around edge of platter. Serves 6.

Cheese-Fish Casserole

¼ cup butter
1½ cups milk
¾ cup cheese
2 tablespoons flour
¼ teaspoon salt

1 pound fillet of sole
   or haddock
¼ teaspoon nutmeg
¼ teaspoon pepper

Melt butter and cheese in warm milk. Add flour which has been mixed with water to form a paste and add to milk mixture and cook until white sauce consistency. Arrange fish slices in buttered baking dish and alternate layers of fish and sauce, sprinkling with spices. Bake 45 minutes at 350°.

Crabmeat Pie

3 cups crabmeat
2/3 cup chili sauce
1 tablespoon lemon juice
1½ teaspoons grated onion
½ teaspoon salt
9-inch unbaked pastry shell
1½ cups cheese sauce

Combine crabmeat, chili sauce, lemon juice, onion and salt. Turn into chilled pastry shell. Add cheese sauce. Sprinkle with paprika. Bake in hot oven at 400° about 50 minutes or until browned and bubbly. Make cheese sauce with thick white sauce and add 1½ cups grated cheese and ½ teaspoon Worcestershire sauce.

Baked Scallops

1 quart scallops
1 green pepper, chopped fine
1½ cups fine bread crumbs
½ teaspoon dry mustard
¼ teaspoon black pepper
1 teaspoon Worcestershire
Dash of tabasco
¼ cup melted butter

Mix the green pepper, bread crumbs, mustard, pepper, Worcestershire and tabasco. Roll the scallops in the melted fat and then in crumb mixture until well coated. Put in greased baking dish large enough so that scallops are not more than three deep. Dot with butter and bake in 350° oven for 30 minutes. Garnish with thin slices of lemon and little parsley. Serves 6.

Scallop Casserole

1 quart scallops	½ pound grated cheese
3 cups very thick white sauce (3 tablespoons flour to 1 fat, 1 cup milk)	1 small bottle stuffed olives
	1 small can pimiento
1 can undiluted tomato soup	1 small can mushrooms

Blanch the scallops; squeeze out the moisture on towel. Cut scallops if large. Add to sauce. Top with buttered crumbs. Bake 1 hour at 350°.

Baked Stuffed Fish Fillets

Fish fillets	Dry bread crumbs
Lemon juice	Salt and pepper
Small oysters	Dash poultry seasoning

Place fillets on greased baking sheet, brush with lemon juice. Sprinkle with salt and pepper. Make a stuffing by draining the oysters and rolling them in the bread crumbs which have been mixed with salt, pepper and poultry seasoning. Arrange the crumbed oysters on the fillets, sprinkle with lemon juice. Cover the stuffing with another fillet and cover this with buttered crumbs. Bake at 375° for 1 hour. One-half pint of oysters will make enough stuffing for 4 servings.

Maine Sardine Casserole Caliente

3 cans (4 oz.) sardines
4 slices bacon, chopped
1 cup raw white rice
1 green pepper, cubed
1 large onion, sliced
1 can (1 lb.) tomatoes

1 can (13¾ oz.)
  chicken broth
1 tablespoon chili
  powder (or more to taste)
Dash tabasco
Dash thyme
Salt and pepper to taste

Drain sardines. Saute bacon until crisp, take from pan and reserve. Stir rice, green pepper and onion into hot bacon fat. Cook 3-4 minutes. Stir in tomatoes, chicken broth and seasonings. Turn mixture into a casserole and fold in 1 can sardines, coarsely broken. Bake, covered, for 45 minutes in 350° oven, stirring several times. Remove cover and arrange remaining whole sardines on top of rice. Continue baking for 15-20 minutes more. Garnish with lemon slices. Serves 6.

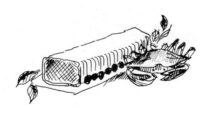

Crab Loaf

½ pound crabmeat
3 eggs, well beaten
½ cup butter, melted
1 teaspoon dry mustard
Dash cayenne

½ teaspoon Worcestershire
1 teaspoon salt
½ cup cracker crumbs
1 cup cream
1 cup milk

Mix all together well and place in greased loaf pan. Bake in 350° oven for 45 minutes, or until firm. Serve hot.

Cheese Baked Sardines and Pasta

2 cans (4 oz.) sardines
1 package (8 oz.) pasta
   shells
1 cup grated sharp cheese
1 can condensed cheese soup

1 large firm tomato,
   thinly sliced
½ cup dairy sour cream
Salt, pepper and dill
   to taste

Drain sardines. Cook pasta according to package instructions. Drain. Combine cooked pasta, cheese, soup, halved slices of tomato, sour cream and seasonings. Mix lightly. Add 1 can sardines broken into coarse pieces. Turn mixture into greased baking dish or casserole. Arrange 1 can whole sardines on top. Bake in 350° oven for 20 minutes. Serve hot with lemon slices. Serves 4-5.

Fisherman's Bake

2 cans (4 oz.) sardines
6 hard-cooked eggs
1 tablespoon prepared
   mustard
¼ cup mayonnaise
½ cup shredded sharp cheese

Dash tabasco
Salt and pepper
¼ pound fresh mushrooms,
   sliced
2 cups medium cream sauce

Drain sardines. Cut eggs in half, lengthwise, remove yolks and reserve whites. Mash yolks with next 5 ingredients. Spoon egg yolk mixture into whites. Place filled eggs and whole sardines in a shallow baking dish. Simmer mushrooms in water to cover until tender. Add mushrooms and few tablespoons of the cooking liquid to cream sauce. Pour sauce over eggs and sardines. Bake at 350° for 15 minutes or until hot and bubbly. Serves 4-6.

PREPARING A MAINE CLAMBAKE

Clambakes are a part of Maine, as are bean suppers and lobster bakes. What could be more appealing than a clambake along the ocean, with the smell of fresh salt air and cool ocean breezes? Clambakes are part of Maine's charm and her heritage.

There are many ways to arrange a clambake, depending on the number of people, materials available and individual fance. But basically the processes are the same: to generate sufficient steam to thoroughly cook the food within a concentrated space. During the cooking process steam is produced by placing wet seaweed on rocks previously heated by a hot fire.

The most popular procedure involves digging a shallow, circular hole in the ground from 8 to 10 inches deep. The diameter depends on the number of persons to be fed: for 20 persons allow a 3 foot circle, 50 persons, a 5 foot circle and on up.

The hole is next lined with smooth hard rocks arranged so the tops are level and close together. After sweeping the rocks clean, place good dry hardwood and kindling wood on top and light it. Keep the fire low for about 2 hours until steam is emmited when water is dropped on the rocks. Quickly remove all burning wood and coals and brush the rocks clean with a green birch brush. Now place a layer of wet seaweed on the clean hot rocks. Place washed clams on top of the seaweed (you'll find a bushel of clams will generously feed 30 persons.) Next place lobsters directly on top of the clams and additional layers of sweet corn, potatoes, frankfurters and potatoes and eggs.

Cover all with a piece of canvas, making certain it is not touching the hot rocks. Let the bake remain about an hour, then check the lobsters near the edges to see if they are done.

The feast begins when the layers of hot sweetcorn, sizzling frankfurters, bright red lobsters and tender, juicy steamed clams are uncovered, and in no time at all, devoured.

Mary Anne's Clam Casserole

2 cups milk
2 cups crumbled unsalted
  crackers
1 pint clams and juice
4 eggs, well beaten

¼ cup minced onions
1 tablespoon minced
  pimiento
1 teaspoon salt
¼ teaspoon pepper

Combine cracker crumbs and milk and let stand for 20 minutes. Add clams which have been ground and juice. Add eggs well beaten, onions, pimiento and seasonings. Pour into greased 2 quart casserole. Bake 40-50 minutes at 350°. Serves 4.

Maine Steamed Clams

Scrub the shells and carefully wash clams free of sand in several waters. Place in large kettle with 2 cups of water. Cover, bring to boiling point and steam until shells open. Serve very hot with side dish of melted butter and a cup of the clam bouillon (liquor from the kettle). Allow 15-20 clams per serving.

Maine Clam Casserole

2 cups clams, with juice
1 cup cracker crumbs
2 tablespoons chopped
  onions
3 eggs, beaten slightly

½ cup milk
1 cup cream style corn
2 tablespoons melted
  butter
Salt and pepper to taste

Combine all ingredients and put into buttered casserole. Bake 45-60 minutes at 350°. Serves 4.

Maine Sea-Burgers

2 cups finely chopped
  clams
1 cup cornflakes
1 egg, well beaten
¼ cup milk

1 tablespoon minced
  onion
1 tablespoon minced
  celery
Salt and pepper to taste

Combine ingredients. Form into patties. Have hot shortening or oil one inch deep in skillet. Fry burgers golden brown and serve piping hot.

Fried Clams

1 egg yolk, beaten	¼ teaspoon salt
½ cup milk	½ cup flour
1 tablespoon melted butter	1 egg white beaten stiff
	24 clams, cleaned

Combine beaten egg yolk and half the milk. Add butter. Add salt to flour, sift together and beat into egg-milk mixture until smooth. Add rest of milk, then fold in stiffly beaten egg white. Drain clams. Dip each clam into batter and fry in deep fat (375°) until golden brown, turning frequently. Drain on absorbent paper. Serve with ketchup. Serves 4.

Maine Clam Pie

1 pie shell, with enough crust to cover	1 tablespoon butter, melted
2 cups clams, chopped fine	½ cup cracker crumbs
¼ cup clam liquor	1 egg, well beaten
Salt and pepper	1 cup milk

Clean the clams and strain the liquor, saving ¼ cup of the liquor. Combine all of the ingredients, season with salt and pepper and pour into a deep pie shell. Cover with upper crust, seal all around the shell and pierce top crust with fork. Bake 1 hour in moderate oven (350°). Serve hot with mashed potatoes.

Scalloped Clams

1 pint clams	1 cup cracker crumbs
4 tablespoons clam liquor	½ cup melted butter
2 tablespoons cream	Salt and pepper

Prepare clams by removing black part and separating soft part from strap and head. Chop strap and head quite fine. Mix melted butter with cracker crumbs and be generous with butter. Spread a thin layer of crumbs in bottom of shallow baking dish which has been well greased. Add ½ of the clams, sprinkle with salt and pepper, add 2 tablespoons liquor, repeat using rest of clams and saving some crumbs for the top. Never use more than two layers. The cream is added last. Bake 30 minutes in a 400° oven.

Maine Coast Clam Fritters

2 eggs (large)	1 cup milk
2 cups shucked raw clams	¼ teaspoon pepper
1 cup flour	½ teaspoon salt

Chop clams very fine. Make batter by beating eggs, add flour gradually. Add milk slowly, salt and pepper, then chopped clams. Stir all together. Drop by spoonfuls into deep hot fat that will color a 1-inch cube of bread golden brown, or have fat at 365° on a fat thermometer. When brown turn and brown on reverse side and serve piping hot.

Browned Clam Hash

½ cup chopped onion
1½ cups finely diced
   cooked potato
1 pint minced clams
2 tablespoons light cream

½ teaspoon salt
Dash pepper
¼ cup butter or
   margarine
Catsup

In large bowl combine onion, potato, clams, cream, salt and pepper; mix well. Melt butter in large skillet, add hash mixture, pressing down firmly with spatula. Cook over medium heat, without stirring, until nicely browned on underside — about 15 minutes. Run spatula around edge to loosen, fold one half over the other and serve with catsup. Serves 4.

Cheesy Clam Casserole

2 cups elbow macaroni,
   cooked and drained
1 can (10½ oz.) Welsh
   Rarebit
1 cup minced clams

½ cup packaged dry
   bread crumbs
2 tablespoons butter
   or margarine, melted

Preheat oven to 350° F. Combine maccaroni, Welsh Rarebit and clams with their liquid in a 1-quart casserole; mix well. Sprinkle top with mixture of bread crumbs and melted butter. Bake, uncovered, 20 minutes or until hot and bubbly. Serves 4.

Clams Poulette

1 pint minced clams	¼ teaspoon nutmeg
¼ cup butter or margarine	Milk
	2 teaspoons lemon juice
¼ cup unsifted flour	1 egg yolk, beaten
¼ teaspoon salt	Buttered toast slices

Drain clams, reserving liquid. In medium saucepan melt butter; remove from heat. Blend in flour, salt and nutmeg. Add enough milk to reserved clam liquid to measure 2 cups. Stir into mixture in saucepan with lemon juice. Over medium heat, bring to boiling, stirring. Remove from heat. Stir a little hot sauce into egg yolk; pour back into saucepan; mix well. Add clams, reheat gently. Serve over toast slices.

Clamburgers

1 cup minced clams	2 tablespoons butter or margarine
1 egg, beaten	
½ cup crushed saltine crackers	Toasted hamburger rolls
	Catsup
¼ teaspoon salt	Lemon wedges

In small bowl, combine clams, egg, crackers, and salt; mix well. Form mixture into 3 patties. In hot butter, in large skillet, saute patties until golden brown on both sides. Serve on hamburger rolls with catsup and lemon wedges. Serves 3.

Clams Supreme

1 pint minced clams	¼ cup catsup
2 tablespoons butter	1 teaspoon Worcestershire
2 tablespoons flour	Toast slices
½ cup light cream	Chopped parsley

Drain clams, reserving ½ cup liquid. Melt butter in medium saucepan; remove from heat. Stir in flour until smooth. Gradually stir in clam liquid, cream, catsup and Worcestershire. Bring to boiling, stirring. Reduce heat and simmer 1 minute. Add clams; reheat. Serve over toast; sprinkle with parsley. Serves 4-6.

Clam Souffle with Shrimp-Newburg Sauce

SOUFFLE

1 tablespoon flour
1 teaspoon dry mustard
Dash salt
1 teaspoon Worcestershire
6 egg yolks, slightly
 beaten
1 can cream-of-mushroom
 soup
1 cup minced clams,
 drained

6 egg whites, room
 temperature
1/8 teaspoon cream of
 tartar

SAUCE

1 can cream-of-shrimp soup
¼ cup light cream
¼ cup sherry
2 egg yolks, beaten
Dash nutmeg

Preheat oven to 350° F. for Souffle. In medium saucepan combine flour, mustard, salt, Worcestershire, egg yolks, and mushroom soup. Cook, stirring constantly, over low heat until mixture is smooth and thick. Add clams; cool slightly. Beat egg whites with cream of tartar until stiff; gently fold in clam mixture. Turn into greased souffle dish. Set dish in hot water. Bake 45-50 minutes. Sauce: In small saucepan, combine soup, cream, sherry and nutmeg; bring to boiling. Remove from heat. Stir a little hot sauce into yolks; pour back in pan and cook, stirring until thickened. Serve sauce hot over souffle. Serves 4.

Clam Tetrazzini

2 tablespoons butter
2 tablespoons flour
1 can cream of mushroom soup
1/3 cup milk
¼ cup sherry

1 cup grated sharp Cheddar cheese
1 pint minced clams
1 package (8 oz.) spaghetti, cooked and drained
½ cup grated Parmesan cheese

Preheat oven to 350° F. In large saucepan, melt butter; remove from heat. Stir in flour until smooth. Stir in soup, milk and sherry. Bring mixture to boiling, stirring. Remove from heat; stir in Cheddar cheese, clams and spaghetti. Turn mixture into shallow baking dish; sprinkle with Parmesan cheese. Bake, uncovered, 20-25 minutes. Serves 6.

Deep Dish Clam and Cornbread Pie

1 cup minced clams
1 can cream of clam stew
½ cup fresh bread crumbs
¼ cup minced onion
Egg
Milk

2 eggs, beaten
1 tablespoon lemon juice
1 package (8 oz.) corn-muffin mix
Parsley

Preheat oven to 400° F. Combine clams, stew, bread crumbs, onion, eggs and lemon juice in casserole. Prepare muffin mix as package label directs, using egg and milk. Spoon batter over clam mixture, covering completely. Bake, uncovered, 30 minutes. To serve garnish with parsley. Makes 4-5 servings.

Stuffed Clams

Cover bottom of dripping pan with rock salt. Arrange 2 quarts large-sized soft-shelled clams on salt, in such a manner that liquor will not run into pan as clams open. Set in hot oven. As soon as shells begin to open, remove clams from shells, and chop. Reserve liquor, and strain. Melt 2 tablespoons butter, add 3 tablespoons flour, stir until well blended and add ¼ cup each of clam liquor and cream. Season highly with lemon juice and cayenne. Moisten clams with sauce, fill shells, sprinkle with grated cheese, cover with buttered, soft, stale bread crumbs, and bake in hot oven 425° F. until crumbs are brown.

Fricassee of Clams

Clean 1 pint clams, chop hard portions finely, and reserve soft portions. Melt 2 tablespoons butter, add chopped clams, 2 tablespoons flour, and pour on gradually ½ cup cream. Strain sauce or not, add soft part of clams, cook 1 minute, season with salt and cayenne, and add 1 egg yolk slightly beaten.

CASCO BAY ISLANDS

The 18 miles of Casco Bay extend from Cape Elizabeth to Cape Small Point. These islands were first discovered by a Captain Prine on one of his trips in search of sassafrass. The "Calendar of Isles" as they are sometimes called were supposed to number one for each day of the year.

Over 250 years ago Colonel Romer, inspecting the islands as an engineer for His Majesty in America reported that: "Said bay is covered from storms that come from ye sea by a multitude of Islands, great and small, there being as many islands as there days in a year.

Casco Bay is filled with the romance of the smuggler and the pirate; the famous Captain Kidd is supposed to have buried untold treasure on Jewell's Island. The story goes that he sighted a frigate just off Long Island and immediately set sail North to avoid it. He anchored at Jewell's Island, took a great kettle filled with jewels and gold ashore and buried it on the southern end of the island under a rock.

In 1840 one man really did find a pot of gold as he was duck hunting one day on the Cedar Ledges, between Ram and Elm Islands. As he climbed on the slimy rocks, his foot slipped into a hole and looking down, he discovered an old copper kettle filled with gold coins. These, he took to Boston and exchanged them for 12 thousand American dollars. Where the treasure was found is now known as Pirate's Gold Pot, visible only at low tide.

Broiled or Sauteed Oysters

1 pint selected oysters	2/3 cup seasoned
¼ cup melted butter	cracker crumbs

Clean oysters and dry between towels. Lift with silver fork by the tough muscle and dip in butter. Then in cracker crumbs which have been seasoned with salt and pepper. Place in buttered wire broiler and broil until juices flow, turning while broiling. Or, put 2 tablespoons butter in hot frying pan, add oysters, brown on one side, then turn and brown on the other. Serves 4.

Oyster Fricassee

1 pint oysters	¼ teaspoon salt
Milk or cream	Few grains cayenne
2 tablespoons butter	1 teaspoon parsley,
2 tablespoons flour	finely chopped
1 egg, slightly beaten	

Parboil oysters and add enough cream to liquor to make a cup. Melt butter, add flour, and pour on gradually hot liquid; stir until thickened and add salt, cayenne, parsley, oysters and egg. If preferred, double amount of flour and omit egg. Serves 4.

Oysters with Bacon

Clean oysters, wrap a thin slice of bacon around each, and fasten with small wooden skewers. Put in broiler, place broiler over dripping pan, and bake in hot oven until bacon is crisp and brown, turning once during cooking. Drain on brown paper.

Deviled Oysters on Half Shells

1 pint oysters	1/8 teaspoon nutmeg
1 tablespoon butter	Few grains cayenne
3 shallots, finely chopped	½ teaspoon prepared mustard
2 tablespoons flour	½ tablespoon Worcestershire
½ cup milk	3 chopped mushroom caps
¼ cup cream	½ teaspoon chopped parsley
½ teaspoon salt	1 egg yolk
Buttered cracker crumbs	

Wash and chop oysters. Cook shallots in butter 3 minutes, add flour, and stir until well blended; then add milk and cream. Bring to boiling point, add oysters and remaining ingredients, except egg yolk and crumbs, and simmer 12 minutes. Add egg yolk, put mixture in deep halves of oyster shells, cover with buttered crumbs, and bake 15 minutes. Serves 6.

Oysters and Macaroni

1 pint oysters
1½ cups boiled macaroni
Salt and pepper

Flour
½ cup buttered crumbs
¼ cup butter

Put a layer of macaroni in bottom of a buttered baking dish, cover with oysters, sprinkle with salt and pepper, dredge with flour, dot over with half the butter; repeat and cover with buttered crumbs. Bake 20 minutes in hot oven 450° F. Serves 4-6.

Scalloped Oysters

1 pint oysters
4 tablespoons oyster liquor
2 tablespoons milk or
cream

½ cup stale bread crumbs
1 cup cracker crumbs
½ cup melted butter
Salt and pepper

Mix bread and cracker crumbs and stir in butter. Put a thin layer in bottom of shallow, buttered baking dish, cover with oysters, and sprinkle with salt and pepper; add half, each, oyster liquor and milk or cream. Repeat and cover top with remaining crumbs. Bake 30 minutes in hot oven 450° F. Never allow more than 2 layers of oysters for Scalloped Oysters; if 3 layers are used, the middle layer will be underdone, while others are properly cooked. If desired, sprinkle each layer with mace or grated nutmeg. Serves 4.

Oyster and Mushroom Casserole

4 tablespoons grated onion	1 pint milk
8 tablespoons butter	½ teaspoon salt
½ pound mushrooms	Dash pepper
6 tablespoons flour	½ teaspoon lemon juice
1 pint oysters	

Cook onion in fat until golden brown. Add mushrooms and cook 5 minutes; add flour and cook slowly 7 minutes. Heat oysters in milk until edges curl. Add this to first mixture and cook until smooth. Place in casserole, cover with buttered crumbs and bake at 400° until crumbs brown.

Scalloped Mussels

Wash 1 quart mussels, cover with hot water and bring quickly to the boil, cook 5-6 minutes to open shells. Drain and remove meat. Combine 2 cups bread crumbs with ¼ cup melted butter. Place in layer of the crumbs in a buttered casserole. Add a layer of mussels, sprinkle with minced green pepper and season with salt, pepper and onion salt. Repeat until crumbs and mussels are used. Pour in enough milk to moisten and sprinkle buttered crumbs on top. Bake 30-40 minutes at 350°. Serves 4.

Panned Mussels

30 mussels in shell
2 tablespoons butter
2 tablespoons flour

½ cup cold water
Salt, pepper and cayenne
Juice of ½ lemon

Remove mussel meat from shells as described in Scalloped Mussels and place in saucepan with butter, seasonings, and lemon juice. Heat slowly. Put cold water in a covered jar, put flour on water. Cover jar tightly and shake vigorously to mix to cream-like consistency. Add slowly to hot mixture, stirring constantly. Bring to a boil and serve.

Mussels on the Half-Shell

4 dozen mussels
1 tablespoon minced onion
1/3 cup water
Juice ½ lemon

3 tablespoons butter
Salt and pepper
1½ teaspoons flour
1 teaspoon parsley

Scrub mussel shells. Place in saucepan with water and lemon juice. Cover and boil 5-6 minutes or until shells open. Discard top shell of each mussel and arrange bottom halves on serving plates. Strain liquid and reduce by boiling. Melt butter in small skillet, blend in flour and seasonings. Add ⅓ cup liquid and bring to boil. Pour over mussels. Serves 4.

OUR FRIEND THE LOBSTER

In the middle of the last century Maine fishermen realized the value of the lobster in supplying out of state markets. Since then this tasty crustaceon has become Maine's trademark.

Our friend the lobster lives in a colony, staying close to Maine's shores. He may venture out of his craigy habitat in search of food, only to learn that others are in search of him.

The fisherman has baited his lobster pot, or traps with oily fish and fish heads, a tasty treat no respectable lobster can forego.

Long age primitive traps were merely hook staffs, but from the modernization of the lobster pot emerged the Parlor Pot. Undesputibly the most effective type of trapping method, the Parlor Pot sits on the ocean bottom with its tasty bait.

How can our friend resist? In he goes after his dinner, and within a few short hours he himself is boiled bright red being dunked in drawn butter for someone else's dinner.

Boiled State of Maine Lobster

Have about 3 inches of boiling water in large kettle. Add 1 to 2 tablespoons salt, depending on width of kettle and number of lobsters being cooked. Plunge live lobsters in, head downward. Cover kettle, bring back to steaming point rapidly and time 17 minutes for 1 pound size or 18-20 minutes for 1¼-1½ pounders. Remove from water and place each lobster on its back. Using a heavy knife or kitchen shears cut each lobster from head to tip of tail. Spread open and remove intestinal vein and small sac just below the head. Crack large claws. Serve hot with small dish of melted butter. If served cold, mayonnaise may be substituted for melted butter.

Lobster Stew

2 cups lobster meat cut in cubes
1 quart milk

4 tablespoons butter
1 cup cream

Melt butter. Add lobster meat and cook 10 minutes. Add scalded milk and cream, season with salt and pepper and serve at once.

Baked Maine Lobster Deluxe

4 fresh lobsters	2 egg yolks
3 small fresh lobsters	1 cup lobster stock
2 tablespoons butter	1 cup toasted bread cubes
½ cup cream	2 tablespoons sherry

Cook lobsters in 3 inches boiling salted water for 15 minutes. Set the 4 large ones to one side, belly up, so juice does not run out of shell. Remove meat from small ones and cut in bit-size pieces. Cook the shells with 1½ cups of water, any juice from the 3 lobsters, a little celery, parsley and seasoning for 15 minutes. Strain. This makes the lobster stock. In a double boiler melt butter, add cream and slightly beaten egg yolks and stir constantly as it thickens. Add lobster stock and cook, stirring constantly until the consistency of cream sauce. Remove from heat, add lobster meat, toasted bread crumbs and sherry. Next split large lobsters. Remove vein, stomach and liver. Cut the thin under-shell from tail so meat shows. Crack large claws. Fill body cavity generously with the lobster mixture. Sprinkle with fine battered bread crumbs. Bake in 500 F oven for 10-12 minutes to heat and brown crumbs. Serve with melted butter.

Maine's own Lobster Roll

Blend two cups cooked chilled lobster meat with two tablespoons mayonnaise. Add ¼ cup finely diced celery, if desired. Mix well and let stand in refrigerator until ready to use. Split and toast 4 hamburger rolls and spread with melted butter. Fill rolls with lobster meat and serve.

Lobster Casserole

3 tablespoons butter
1 pound cooked lobster
   meat
3 tablespoons flour
3/4 teaspoon dry mustard

3 slices white bread
   (crusts removed)
2 cups rich milk
Salt and pepper to taste

Cut lobster into bite sized pieces and cook slowly in butter to start the pink color. Do not cook too long or too fast or it will toughen. Combine flour with seasonings and sprinkle over lobster; add milk slowly stirring to blend. Cook, stirring gently, until thickened. Add bread torn into small irregular pieces. Pour into greased casserole; top with buttered crumbs and bake about 30 minutes at 350 F until bubbly and brown. If desired, 2-3 tablespoons of sherry may be added when the bread is stirred in.

Tangy Maine Lobster

2 cups lobster meat
1/3 cup butter
1 teaspoon Worcestershire

1 tablespoon lemon juice
1 teaspoon dry mustard
Salt and pepper to taste

Place all ingredients, except lobster, in top part of double boiler. Melt over hot water; stir to blend well. Cut lobster in small pieces; add to mixture and cook 6 minutes. Serve on toast with lemon wedges. Serves 4.

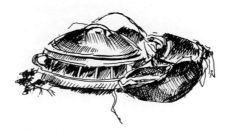

Lobster Casserole Au Gratin
with Herb Seasoning

1 pound clear lobster meat, cut in pieces	¼ cup buttered bread crumbs
1½ tablespoon butter	½ cup grated sharp cheese
2 tablespoons flour	½ tablespoon minced parsley
Salt and pepper	
¼ teaspoon dry mustard	¼ teaspoon mixed herb seasoning
1/8 teaspoon curry powder	
1 cup thin cream	

Place lobster pieces in buttered shallow baking dish, sprinkle with salt and pepper. Make a tangy cream sauce of the butter, flour, cream, salt, pepper, dry mustard, curry powder and half of the grated sharp cheese. Pour sauce over lobster. Sprinkle with buttered crumbs which have been combined with rest of cheese, the minced parsley and herb seasoning. Bake in moderate (350) oven for 25-30 minutes.

Lobster Wiggle

2 cups lobster	24 crisp crackers
2 cups cooked peas	Paprika
2 cups white sauce	

Heat lobster and peas in white sauce. Salt and pepper to taste. Serve on crackers and sprinkle with paprika.

Live Baked Lobster with Clam Dressing

4 live lobsters
6 cups cracker crumbs (scant)
1 teaspoon dry mustard
1 teaspoon poultry seasoning
1 large egg

1 cup cream or evaporated milk, undiluted
1 pint clams
Lobster liver
2 oz. sherry
Salt and pepper to taste

Prepare live lobsters. Beginning at the mouth make a deep incision and with sharp cut draw knife quickly through body and entire length of tail. Remove stomach, intestinal vein and liver. Save livers for dressing. Put clams through meat grinder, saving juice. Mix together cracker crumbs, salt, pepper, mustard, poultry seasoning. Add unbeaten eggs, lobster livers, cream, sherry and clams. Mix well. Add clam liquor. Mixture should be quite moist. Stuff lobsters and dot with butter. Place in 400 F oven and bake until shells are pink and then place under broiler and brown stuffing. Serve with drawn butter.

Lobster Delight

Mash yolks of 4 hard-boiled eggs and mix them with 2 tablespoons of butter rubbed into a paste. Put 1 pint of cream into a double boiler and when it is scalded stir in egg yolks and butter until smooth. Season with salt, black and cayenne pepper, a dash of nutmeg and allspice. Add 1 quart of lobster and simmer 10 minutes. At time of serving add 3 tablespoons of hot sherry or Madeira wine.

Lobster A La Newburg

3 cups cooked lobster	1½ cups cream
3 tablespoons butter	3 egg yolks, well beaten
1½ cups Madeira wine	¼ teaspoon salt
Dash of cayenne	

Cut lobster meat into large pieces and heat slowly in butter about 5 minutes. Add wine and simmer until wine is almost all reduced. Beat cream into egg yolks, add to butter and season. Cook, stirring constantly until thickened. Do not boil. Serve at once.

Lobster Thermidor

2 lobsters	2 tablespoons dry mustard
4 tablespoons butter	2/3 cup sherry
½ cup fresh mushrooms	½ cup buttered cracker
2 cups medium white sauce	crumbs

Boil lobsters; split length wise and clean. Take out solid meat and cut in pieces. Melt butter in frying pan, add sliced mushrooms and saute for 3 minutes. Add white sauce and mustard and blend well. Put in sherry and lobster meat, mixing thoroughly. Remove from pan and place in lobster shells. Cover with buttered cracker crumbs. Bake until crumbs are browned. Serve hot. Serves 4.

Scalloped Lobster

1½ cups lobster meat	½ teaspoon prepared
1 cup soft bread crumbs	mustard
1 cup top milk or	1 tablespoon lemon juice
thin cream	Few drops onion juice
1 egg, well beaten	½ teaspoon salt — pepper
2 tablespoons melted	if desired
butter or margarine	Crumbs for topping

Mix in the order given. Put into greased baking dish and cover with buttered crumbs. Bake 30 minutes in a moderate oven (350 F.). Serves 4.

Lobster Bisque

Remove meat from a 2-pound boiled lobster. Add 2½ cups cold water to the shell and clams and cook 25 minutes. Drain and reserve 2 cups stock. Cut lobster meat in small pieces. Add lobster and stock to 2 cups medium white sauce. Serve piping hot.

(White Sauce — 1 cup milk, 2 tablespoons flour and 2 table-spoons butter or other fat.) The flavor secret is in cooking the lobster shell to make stock, getting the fat and small bits of meat.

Lobster Cutlet

3 pounds boiled lobster
2 tablespoons butter
2 tablespoons flour
½ cup milk
Bread crumbs

¼ teaspoon grated nutmeg
1 teaspoon lemon juice
1 egg
Salt and pepper to taste

Cut lobster meat as fine as possible. Cream butter and flour in saucepan; add milk and cook until thick. Add salt, pepper, lemon juice and nutmeg, mixing well. While hot, add lobster and spread on plate to cool, then shape into cutlet forms, dip in egg and bread crumbs. Fry until golden brown in hot fat and drain well before serving. Garnish with lemon, parsley, aspic or olives.

Fricassee of Lobster and Mushrooms

2-pound lobster, cooked
¼ cup butter
¾ pound mushrooms
Few drops onion juice
2 tablespoons sherry

¼ cup flour
1½ cups milk
Salt
Paprika

Remove lobster meat from shell and cut in strips. Cook butter with mushrooms broken in pieces and onion juice 3 minutes; add flour and pour milk on gradually. Add lobster meat, season with sherry, salt and paprika. Serves 6.

Planked Live Lobster

Live lobster
Olive oil or melted
 butter
Julienne potatoes
Salt and pepper

Sliced tomatoes, peeled
 and chilled
Sliced cucumbers
Parsley
Lemon juice

Split a live lobster and place in dripping pan, brushing with oil or butter. Bake 15 minutes in hot oven (450 F.). Remove to plank, garnish with potatoes, tomatoes, cucumbers, and parsley. Over lobster pour melted butter seasoned with salt, pepper and lemon juice.

Creamed Lobster with Tomato

2 tablespoons butter
1 tablespoon chopped
 onion
2/3 cup hot, boiled rice
1¼ cups lobster diced
¼ cup tomato sauce

Few grains soda
Salt
Celery Salt
Cayenne
½ cup heavy cream

Cook butter with onion 5 minutes, stirring constantly. Add lobster, rice and cream. When heated, add tomato sauce (to which soda has been added) and season highly with salt, celery salt and cayenne. Serves 6.

Fried Lobster

Remove cooked lobster meat from shell. Use tail meat, divided in fourths, and large pieces of claw meat. Sprinkle with salt, pepper, and lemon juice; dip in crumbs, egg and again in crumbs; fry in deep fat (385 F.), drain, and serve with tartare sauce.

Lobster A La Muisset

2 live lobsters (1½ pounds each)	1 teaspoon salt
1 tablespoon finely chopped shallot	1 1/3 cups Brown Stock
	2/3 cup stewed and strained tomatoes
3 tablespoons chopped carrot	3 tablespoons cooking sherry
6 tablespoons butter	Finely chopped chives
2 sprigs thyme	2 red peppers from
½ bay leaf	pepper sauce

Cut lobster in pieces for serving, remove intestinal vein and lady, and crack large claws. Cook shallot and carrot in 2 table-spoons butter 10 minutes, stirring constantly that carrots may not burn. Add thyme, bay leaf, peppers, salt, stock, tomatoes and sherry. Add lobster. Cook 15 minutes. Remove lobster to serving dish. Thicken sauce with flour and remaining butter cooked together. Pour sauce over lobster and sprinkle with finely chopped chives. Serves 4.

Creamed Lobster and Oysters

1 pint oysters	¼ cup butter
2 cups lobster meat	1/3 cup flour
1½ cups cold water	¾ cup cream
1 stalk celery	½ teaspoon beef extract
1 slice onion	Worcestershire sauce
Salt and paprika	Lemon juice

Clean and parboil oysters; drain and add to liquor body bones and touch claw meat from lobster, with water, celery and onion. Cook slowly until stock is reduced to 1 cup, and strain. Make sauce of butter, flour, strained stock and cream. Add oysters and lobster meat, diced or cut in strips; then add seasonings. If desired, omit beef extract, Worcestershire, and lemon juice and add 1½ tablespoons sauterne. Serves 8 or more.

Lobster Farci

1 cup chopped cooked lobster meat	1 cup thin White Sauce
Yolks 2 hard-cooked eggs	Slight grating nutmeg
½ tablespoon chopped parsley	1/3 cup buttered crumbs
	Salt and pepper

To lobster meat add egg yolks rubbed to paste, parsley, sauce and seasonings to taste. Fill lobster shells, cover with buttered crumbs, and bake until crumbs are brown. Serves 4.

Lobster Souffle

2 cups cooked lobster
¼ teaspoon salt
1/8 teaspoon paprika
2 tablespoons lemon
   juice

½ cup bread crumbs.
½ cup milk
3 egg yolks
3 egg whites

Cut lobster meat into small pieces and add seasonings. Cook bread crumbs in milk 5 minutes, add lobster and egg yolks which have been beaten till thick and lemon-colored; then cut and fold in egg whites, beaten stiff. Turn into buttered dish, set in pan of hot water, and bake in moderate oven (350 F.) till firm.

Spanish Lobster

2 pounds cooked lobster
2½ cups cold water
1 slice carrot
1 slice onion
Sprig of parsley
1 stalk celery
4 tablespoons butter
4 tablespoons flour

6 slices broiled tomato
½ cup heavy cream
2 egg yolks
1 tablespoon lemon juice
½ teaspoon salt
¼ teaspoon paprika
1/8 teaspoon pepper
½ cup boiled rice

Cut lobster meat in small pieces. Put bones and small claws in pan; add water, carrot, onion, parsley and celery. Bring to boiling point and cook until reduced to 1½ cups. Strain and pour gradually on butter and flour cooked together. Bring to boiling point, add cream, egg yolks and lobster. Season with lemon juice, salt, paprika, and pepper. Put layer of rice in buttered casserole. Fill with lobster mixture and top with tomato slices, brushed over with melted butter and seasoned with salt and pepper.

THE SHIPWRECKS OF CAPE ELIZABETH

The treacherous rocks surrounding Cape Elizabeth were the scene of many shipwrecks in the days preceding adequate coastal warnings. The wreck of the BOHEMIAN in 1864 was the most disasterous shipwreck in Cape history, claiming 42 lives.

Fog hung over the calm sea that eventful February night when the vessel struck Alden's Rock and went aground off Staple's Cove. Panic arose from the confusion in the darkness, resulting in overturned lifeboats and drownings. The floundering ship went down in only 30 feet of water. Ironically, if it had been low tide the passengers and crew might have almost been able to walk safely to shore.

The BAY STATE went off course and struck McKenney's Point in the impenetrable fog of the early morning of September 23, 1916. All 250 passengers and crew were rescued by the life-saving station at Two Lights, and the ship remained on the rocks for months. It was felt that the vessel would surely break up any moment under the ceaselessly pounding heavy seas. But there she remained, to become a great sight for curiosity seekers. The ship finally broke up in a storm and lay on a reef so close to shore that it was possible to go aboard without getting wet. Apparently a number of people succeeded in doing just that, for today pieces of wood, carpeting and fixtures from the fine ship can still be found in homes throughout Maine.

Deviled Shrimp Casserole

2 #1 cans shrimp	1 cup milk
4 tablespoons butter	2 tablespoons chopped
2 tablespoons flour	Parsley
¼ teaspoon salt	1 tablespoon lemon juice
½ teaspoon dry mustard	1 cup soft bread crumbs
Dash cayenne pepper	2 tablespoons melted butter

Shred shrimp, saving 2 or 3 whole shrimp to garnish each serving. Melt butter, blend into flour, salt, mustard and cayenne pepper. Add milk, stirring constantly, and cook until thickened. Add parsley, lemon juice and shrimp. Place in individual baking dishes or casserole. Sprinkle with bread crumbs which have been mixed with the melted butter. Bake in a moderate oven about 15 minutes, or until crumbs are browned. Makes 6 servings.

Shrimp Wiggle

2 cups shrimp	24 crisp crackers
2 cups cooked peas	Paprika
2 cups white sauce	

Heat shrimp and peas in white sauce. Salt and pepper to taste. Serve on crackers and sprinkle with paprika.

Shrimp and Cauliflower Casserole

Medium-sized cauliflower, cooked until tender. Then arrange in casserole a layer of cauliflower and a layer of shrimp. Continue in this manner, then cover with cheese sauce, as follows:

3 tablespoons butter
3 tablespoons flour
1½ cups milk

½ cup strong cheese, cut fine

Cover with cracker crumbs, sprinkle with paprika. Bake until brown.

Creamed Shrimp, New England Style

1 can (15 oz.) Clam Chowder, undiluted
¼ cup butter or margarine
¼ cup flour
1 cup light cream
1 tablespoon chopped parsley

Dash dried thyme leaves
Dash dry rosemary leaves
1 teaspoon salt
1/8 teaspoon pepper
1 pound cooked shrimp
½ cup dry sherry
6 baked patty shells

Place chowder in electric blender container. Blend, covered at low speed, until smooth. In medium saucepan melt butter; remove from heat. Stir in flour until smooth. Gradually add cream, parsley, thyme, rosemary, salt and pepper. Stir in chowder. Over medium heat, bring mixture to boiling, stirring constantly. Reduce heat; cook, stirring until mixture has thickened — about 3 minutes. Spoon mixture in patty shells and serve. Makes 6 servings.

Shrimp Newburg

2 cups cooked shrimp	Dash cayenne
¼ cup butter or margarine	Dash nutmeg
2½ tablespoons flour	I pint coffee cream
¾ teaspoon salt	2 egg yolks, beaten
2-3 tablespoons sherry	Toast points or patty shells

Melt butter; blend in flour and seasonings. Add cream and sherry gradually and cook until thickened and smooth, stirring constantly. Stir a little of the hot sauce into slightly beaten egg yolks, then add to sauce stirring constantly. Add shrimp and let heat. Serve immediately on toast points or home made pastry shells.

Deviled Shrimp En Coquille

¼ cup melted butter	I pound shrimp meat
½ cup finely chopped celery	1¼ cups crushed salted crackers
½ green pepper, minced	I teaspoon dry mustard
2 tablespoons minced parsley	Salt and pepper
	1/3 cup evaporated milk

Melt butter in saucepan; in it cook chopped vegetables and the shrimp, stirring to break shrimp a little. Add other ingredients. Form mixture into balls and place in greased shells or individual casseroles. Top with buttered crumbs and bake 10-15 minutes at 400° to heat through and brown crumbs.

Adelaide's Shrimp Gumbo

1 pound shrimp meat	Salt and pepper to taste
½ pound fresh mushrooms	2 cans condensed cream soup
2-3 tablespoons butter	1 can waterchestnuts
1 tablespoon lemon juice	2 tablespoons sherry wine

Peel and slice mushrooms, season with salt, pepper and lemon juice. Cook in skillet with butter 3-4 minutes. Push mushrooms to one side and add shrimp. Cook 1-2 minutes (until they curl). Add 2 cans of soup (mushroom, celery, or vegetable). Heat thoroughly. Thin, if necessary, with milk or cream. Add sliced waterchestnuts and sherry. Serve very hot on steamed rice.

Shrimp Divan

2 10 oz. packages frozen broccoli	1 can cream of celery soup
1 pound raw shrimp meat	1 cup salad dressing
Salt and pepper	1 tablespoon lemon juice
Ac'cent	½ cup shredded cheese
Fish blend herbs	1 cup buttered crumbs

Arrange broccoli in greased 7" x 11" baking pan. Cover with the shrimp. Sprinkle with salt, pepper, Ac'cent and a dash of fish blend herbs. Combine soup, mayonnaise, lemon juice and cheese. Stir together and pour over the shrimp and broccoli. Top with buttered crumbs. Bake 40 minutes at 350°. *Note*: Crumbs may be fine dry bread, fine fresh bread, cornflake crumbs or package stuffing — mix with 3 tablespoons melted butter.

Shrimp Sandwich Filling

2 cups cooked shrimp meat
1 8 oz. cream cheese
Salt, pepper, herbs
¼ to ½ teaspoon sugar

Dash of Worcestershire
¼ teaspoon Ac'cent
Mayonnaise to mix

Mash cream cheese and shrimp together. Add seasonings to taste and enough mayonnaise or salad dressing to reach desired spreading consistency. Use as a spread for crackers, sandwiches or finger rolls.

Maine Shrimp Pate

1 pound shrimp meat
2 tablespoons butter
Salt and pepper
¼ teaspoon Ac'cent
¼ teaspoon herbs (fish)

1 package frozen peas
(10 oz.)
1 can mushroom soup
2 cups well seasoned
mashed potato

Cook shrimp in butter for a minute or two. Add seasonings and place in bottom of greased shallow casserole. Combine peas and mushroom soup and spread over shrimp. Top with mashed potato, placed over the entire top or in a ring around the edges, with a small opening at the center. Bake 30 minutes at 350°.

Beulah's Shrimp Bake

6 slices bread	3 eggs
½ pound sliced American cheese	½ teaspoon salt
2 cups shrimp	½ teaspoon prepared mustard
2½ cups milk	½ teaspoon paprika

Alternate layers of bread, cheese and shrimp in a well buttered 1½ quart casserole, having cheese on top. Beat eggs slightly, add seasonings and milk. Pour over the layered ingredients. Bake 1-1¼ hours at 325°. *Note*: This can be made up ahead and wait in the refrigerator for baking time.

Shrimp and Deviled Egg Casserole

12 deviled egg halves	1 can cream of celery soup
½ pound Maine shrimp	
1 tablespoon butter	1 cup diced cheddar cheese
1 4 oz. can mushroom pieces	1/3 cup milk

Place deviled egg halves in bottom of a Pyrex utility dish. Put shrimp (which have been cooked 1 minute with the butter) over the eggs. Scatter mushrooms and juice over shrimp. Combine soup, milk and cheese in saucepan and heat until cheese melts. Pour over other ingredients, top with buttered crumbs and bake about 25 minutes at 350°.

Baked Shrimp

2 cups shrimp meat	Salt and pepper
2 eggs	2 cups cornflake crumbs
¼ cup water	Oil

Dry shrimp on paper towels. Dip into crumbs, then eggs slightly beaten with water, then into crumbs again. Place on well oiled baking pan so they do not touch, sprinkle with salt and pepper. Turn over with a broad spatula so that both sides will be oiled. Bake at 450° about 6-8 minutes. Serve with your favorite sauce.

Curried Shrimp — The Easiest

2 cups shrimp	3 tablespoons ketchup
1 can cream of celery soup	2 cups boiled rice
½ cup milk	Salt and pepper to taste
2 tablespoons butter	2 tablespoons sherry
½ teaspoon curry powder	

Combine all ingredients. Pour into greased 2 quart casserole. Top with buttered crumbs. Bake 20-30 minutes at 425°.

Boiled Maine Shrimp

Break heads from 2 pounds of fresh Maine shrimp. Place in kettle with 3 cups of water. Bring to boil and time 6 minutes. Cool and peel shells from meat.

Note: This is the starting point for dishes calling for cooked shrimp — you have to plan on getting about half of what you start with. In a word, two pounds will get you one — or about 2 cups of meat. Also, Maine shrimps are so tender that they can easily be overcooked. It is easier to remove from shell raw (cut under shell with scissors), then cook them 2-3 minutes in ¼ to ½ cup of water.

Shrimp Stuffed Peppers

4 large green peppers
2 cups cooked shrimp, cut
½ cup minced onion
2 tablespoons butter
1 teaspoon Worcestershire

Salt and pepper
1½ cups cooked rice
1 cup tomato puree
2/3 cup buttered crumbs

Cut tops from peppers and remove seeds. Serve whole or cut in half, lengthwise. Simmer in 2 cups of boiling water for 5 minutes and drain. Combine remaining ingredients, except buttered crumbs and fill peppers. Top with crumbs and bake in a casserole with ½ cup water 25-30 minutes at 375°. *Note*: If you cut the peppers in half, prepare more buttered crumbs for topping.

Jambalayah Maine Style

2 tablespoons butter	2½ cups canned tomatoes
1 tablespoon flour	1½ cups water
½ pound cooked ham	1 large onion, chopped
1 large green pepper, diced	½ clove garlic, minced
	1 tablespoon minced parsley
2 cups cooked shrimp	¾ cup uncooked rice

Preheat electric skillet to 350°. Melt butter, stir in flour; add diced green pepper and coarsely diced ham. Cook, stirring, for 5 minutes. Add shrimp, tomatoes and water, onion, garlic and parsley. Add salt and pepper as needed. Bring to the boiling point, then add the raw rice. Reduce heat to 200° or 225° and simmer 30 minutes or until rice is tender and has absorbed most of the liquid.

Baked Maine Shrimp Cheese Puff

½ pound cooked shrimp meat	2 cups milk
4 slices buttered bread	¼ teaspoon dry mustard
½ point cheese, grated	Salt and pepper to taste
3 eggs, beaten	

Cut shrimps in 2 or 3 pieces. Butter bread slices and dice in ½ inch cubes. Put half the bread cubes into buttered casserole; spread with half the shrimps and sprinkle with half the cheese. Repeat. Beat eggs slightly. Beat in seasonings and milk. Pour custard over other ingredients and top with a little reserved cheese. Bake 40-50 minutes at 350°. Serves 4 or 5.

Creamed Shrimps with Curacao

1 cup Cream Sauce	¼ teaspoon paprika
¼ teaspoon celery salt	Few gratings nutmeg
¼ cup walnut meats	1 cup shrimps, cooked
½ teaspoon orange curacao	

Season sauce with salt, celery salt, paprika and nutmeg. Add shrimps, cut in halves. Bring to boiling point and add walnut meats, broken in pieces and curacao. Serves 4 to 6.

Shrimps Louisiana Style

2 tablespoons butter	2/3 cup heavy cream
1 teaspoon chopped onion	½ teaspoon salt
2/3 cup cooked shrimps	¼ teaspoon celery salt
2/3 cup hot, boiled rice	3 tablespoons tomato
Few grains cayenne	catsup, if desired

Cook butter with onion 5 minutes, stirring constantly. Add shrimps, rice, and cream. When thoroughly heated add salt, celery salt, cayenne and tomato catsup. Serves 4 to 6.

Shrimps A La Newburg

1 pint shrimps
3 tablespoons butter
1 teaspoon lemon juice
1 teaspoon flour
Salt and pepper

½ cup cream
2 egg yolks, slightly beaten
2 tablespoons sherry

Clean shrimps and cook 3 minutes in 2 tablespoons butter. Add lemon juice and cook 1 minute. Melt 1 tablespoon butter, add flour and cream; when thickened, add egg yolks, shrimps, and sherry. Season and heat. Serves 6.

Sautéed Shrimp

Boil shrimps in salted water 20 minutes or until shells turn pink. Cool in water in which they were boiled. Shell and saute lightly in melted butter. Pour butter over shrimps. If desired, sprinkle with finely chopped parsley.

THE WOODS

Maine has long stood out for her rich land and abundant forest. In the days beyond the memory of man, three Indians of the land of the Algonquins sought and found the Great Spirit, called Glooskap. One was a vain fellow, who though tall, made himself taller by placing fur in his moccasins and tail turkey feathers in his hair. He was and wished to be loved by the squaws. When he stood before Gloospak, he asked that he might be taller than any Indian in the land. The second was a lazy fellow. He wished that he might live forever and do no work. The third wished to have good health and to live to a very old age.

Now, Glooskap summoned Cuhkw, the Earthquake to his side and whispered into his ear. His face was clouded with dislike of the selfish Indian's requests. In a moment there was a terrible roar, Earthquake departed, and in an instant the tall Indian's feet were caught in the earth and he became a pine tree; another Indian's feet were likewise caught and he became a cedar, the third was metamophosed into a pine.

To this day you may see the tail feathers of the turkey on top of the pine tree as it waves in the wind. It is the vain Indian calling your attention to his beauty. And the Indians say that Glooskap gave each his wish, the first became the tallest in the land, the second will remain forever in the land, and the third will live long in health until men cut him down.

And from these trees came the great forests of the world.

Chicken A La Yorkshire

Cut chicken as for frying. Wash and fry in a cloth, then dip in either melted butter or fat from fried pork. Salt and pepper the pieces, then roll in bread or cracker crumbs. Put in baking pan in two layers, baste with melted butter and part water (or baste with pork fat, if used). Bake till thoroughly done, then place chicken on hot platter and cover all with thickened gravy, unstrained.

Italian Chicken

1 chicken	1 small onion, thinly sliced
1½ pints water	3 teaspoons cornstarch
½ cup olive oil	Salt and pepper
1 egg yolk	

Cut the chicken in pieces as for fricassee; cook till tender in just enough water to cover it adding salt and pepper when about half done. Remove from pan and let stand cold; then dry each piece thoroughly. Heat cup of olive oil in a shallow frying pan, add the onion and when smoking hot, put in the chicken, a little at a time and cook golden brown. When cooked, add remaining oil, 1½ cups liquor from chicken, bring to boiling point and thicken with cornstarch rubbed smooth with a little water. Cook 5 minutes and just before serving add the egg yolk and more seasoning, if required. Pour sauce over chicken.

Potted Chicken

Cut up a chicken as for fricassee and to each pound of meat allow 2 tablespoons of flour, ½ teaspoon salt (very scant), and a dash of pepper. Mix thoroughly and roll each piece of meat in the mixture. Pack closely in a large bean pot and cover with boiling water. Bake 3½ hours. Cover after 10-15 minutes, but not before it boils.

Chicken Loaf

1 fowl	2 tablespoons granulated
2 hard-cooked eggs	gelatin
Seasoning to taste	1/3 cup cold water

Boil chicken in sufficient water to cover, till meat is ready to fall from the bones. Cook, strain, and continue to cook the liquor until reduced to 3 cups. Remove all skin and bones from the chicken and lay the meat in a mould, light and dark meat alternately, adding the hard-cooked eggs cut in slices. Season the liquor and add to it the gelatin that has been soaked 5 minutes in ⅓ cup of cold water. When thoroughly dissolved, pour over the meat and set aside to chill.

Curried Chicken

4 tablespoons butter or
  margarine
3 tablespoons flour
1 tablespoon curry powder
Salt and pepper
2 cups cooked chicken,
  diced

2 cups milk or chicken
  broth
1 teaspoon onion juice
½ sour apple or 1 table-
  spoon lemon juice

Melt the butter, add flour and curry powder and cook 5 minutes; then pour in milk or stock and stir constantly till the sauce boils. Add the onion juice, chicken and seasoning and heat thoroughly. If apple is used, chop finely and add as soon as the sauce boils; if lemon is used, do not add to sauce until time of serving. Serve with boiled rice in separate dish.

Fried Chicken

1 chicken
Salt, pepper, flour

Cold water
½ cup oil

Remove pinfeathers and oil sac, wash and then cut off the legs, wings and pieces from body. Dip each piece into the water and then into the flour, salt and pepper which has been sifted together, and dry each piece. Heat the oil in a frying pan and cook the pieces of chicken slowly, turning often while cooking. Keep hot until all pieces are done and serve with white sauce or brown gravy.

Fried Chicken, Rumford Style

1 tender chicken	1 green pepper
Salt and pepper to taste	2 large tomatoes
1 clove garlic	5 tablespoons shortening

Wash and dry chicken, then cut in pieces for serving and sprinkle with salt and pepper. Heat shortening or oil in frying pan, add clove of garlic and green pepper, cut in small pieces. When garlic turns brown remove from frying pan and put in chicken, fry till brown, then cover closely and allow to simmer until ready. Just before covering chicken, add tomatoes, peeled and cut in small pieces.

Fricassee Chicken

1 good-sized chicken	1 tablespoon butter
Few slices salt pork	2 tablespoons flour
1 small onion	Few mushrooms, if desired
Boiling water to cover	Chopped parsley
Salt and pepper	

Cut chicken in good size pieces and wipe with a damp cloth. Cut pork small and fry in saucepan until fat runs freely, then mix with chicken and cook until slightly colored, but not browned. Place the tougher parts of the bird at bottom of pan, then add onion and cover with boiling water. Cover closely and cook very slowly until tender, adding seasoning after 1 hour. A few minutes before serving, remove meat from pan and thicken gravy with butter and flour rubbed together. Cook 5 minutes and pour over meat and sprinkle with parsley.

Braised Duck

1 good-sized duck	1 sliced onion
¼ pound fat salt pork	1 bay leaf
1 carrot, diced	Salt, cayenne and parsley

Cut the pork in small pieces and fry; add the vegetables, bay leaf and parsley and cook 5 minutes. Add duck, either trussed or for roasting or cut into joints. Cook in the fat till browned; then place in baking dish or casserole. Pour vegetables and fat over meat and add 3 cups boiling water. Cover closely and cook in moderate oven until tender, adding more water if necessary. Dish the bird and thicken the gravy with 2 tablespoons each of flour and butter rubbed smoothly together. Season highly and serve with currant jelly or apple sauce.

Chicken Mould

1 cup cold chicken	1 cup chicken stock or
Seasoning	½ stock and ½ milk
1 egg	2 teaspoons gelatin

Chop or pass the chicken through food chopper; add seasonings and egg, yolk and white beaten separately. Dissolve the gelatin in the stock and add to chicken. Turn into a mould. When set, turn out and slice thinly. Garnish with olives.

Chicken Chartreuse

1 cup cooked, cold chicken	1 cup chicken stock or ½ cup stock and ½ cup cream
Salt and pepper	
Little grated lemon rind	1 tablespoon granulated gelatin
1 egg	

Mince the chicken finely, pass through a sieve and season to taste. Soak the gelatin for 10 minutes in cold stock or stock and cream, then heat to boiling point. When gelatin is dissolved, strain and pour over chicken. Add lightly beaten egg yolk, then egg white beaten to a stiff froth. When partly cooked, turn into a mould and put aside until very cold and set. Unmould and cut in thin slices.

Maine Chicken A La Jet

2-3 pounds cut-up chicken	1 envelope dehydrated onion soup
1 large sheet heavy-duty foil, buttered	3 tablespoons apple juice and sherry wine

Butter a large piece of foil lightly. Spread half the package of soup on foil. Arrange chicken meat on top and sprinkle remaining soup over meat. Add liquids. Fold foil over meat, turning in ends to seal completely. Bake in 375° oven, 1-1½ hours, depending on chicken parts used. Serves 4-6.

Blushing Hawaiian Chicken

2-3 pounds breasts and legs
1 cup flour
2 teaspoons salt
¼ teaspoon pepper
2 teaspoons paprika
¼ pound margarine

Mix flour, salt, pepper and paprika in paper bag. Place margarine in pan and melt slowly. Shake the chicken in bag with flour mixture and coat thoroughly. Place chicken, skin side down, in single layer in hot margarine. Bake 45 minutes, then turn and cover with following mixture:

1 can whole cranberry sauce
1 can crushed pineapple
½ cup brown sugar

Push chicken to one side in pan and place favorite biscuit recipe in gravy made by chicken cooking in the margarine. Return to oven and bake 15 minutes or until biscuits are lightly browned.

Potato Chip Chicken

1 2½-3 pound chicken, cut up
2 cups crushed potato chips
¼ teaspoon garlic salt
1/3 cup cooking oil

Line shallow pan or cookie sheet with aluminum foil, greased. Combine crushed chips and seasonings. Dip chicken in oil, then roll in chip mixture. Place pieces in pan skin side up and bake 375° for 1 hour without turning. Serves 4.

Skillet Chicken

1 2/3 pound cut up chicken	½ cup cooking oil
2/3 cup flour	1 cup onion rings
1 teaspoon salt	1 green pepper
½ teaspoon pepper	2 (8 oz.) cans tomato
½ teaspoon garlic salt	sauce

Rinse chicken pieces in cold water, drain and dry. Combine flour, salt, pepper and garlic salt in paper bag. Shake 3-4 pieces of chicken in bag at a time to coat evenly. Heat oil in heavy skillet, and brown chicken on both sides. Arrange onion and green pepper rings over the top. Pour on tomato sauce. Cover skillet and simmer 30-40 minutes. Skillet 420° to brown, 340° to simmer. Serves 4-5.

Barbecued Chicken

2 2½ pound frying chickens	¼ teaspoon mustard
2 tablespoon sugar	2 cups vinegar
1 tablespoon flour	1 cup water
Red pepper	Black pepper and salt

Cut chickens in pieces, arrange in heavy pan, sprinkle with dry ingredients, add liquids, and cover closely. Cook slowly until tender. Put under broiler and cook until liquid is used, basting frequently.

Maine-ly Chicken Casserole

Split breasts of 2 1½ pound chickens, wash and dry the breasts and 4 legs. Put in hot skillet 3 tablespoons butter, add chicken. Brown well on all sides 10-15 minutes. Mix well in bowl:

2 cups water	1 (8 oz.) can small
6 tablespoons flour	boiled onion
1 (10½ oz.) can cream	4 tablespoons dry ready-
of mushroom soup	made poultry stuffing
¼ teaspoon salt	8-10 raw carrot slices

Arrange chicken in casserole. Pour over the above mixture. Make sure carrot sticks are placed deep in the liquids for proper cooking. Bake in 400° oven 1 hour and 45 minutes. Cover for first hour then remove cover for remaining 45 minutes to brown and crisp top. Serves 6-8.

Roast Duck (Wild)

Let stand in warm room until chill is completely off. Dress, clean, stuff with sliced apple or onion, and truss. Sprinkle with salt and pepper, cover breast with 2 very thin slices fat salt pork. Bake 15-30 minutes in very hot oven (450°), basting every 5 minutes with fat in pan. Remove apple or onion. For very rare duck, roast 12-20 minutes, according to size.

Chicken Newburgh

Cut up and wash a 3 pound chicken. Put into 2 quart kettle and add 3 cups cold water. To this add 1 onion, cut up fine, 1 teaspoon salt, ½ teaspoon pepper. Cook 1 hour, starting on high until boiling, then turn to low. When hour is up strain liquid into separate kettle and leave chicken in platter to cool before removing bones and skin. Skim off extra fat from liquid. Add to liquid:

1 can cream of mushroom soup	1 can (1½ oz.) Parmesan cheese
1 teaspoon Worcestershire	½ teaspoon garlic salt
½ teaspoon salt	

After stirring mixture, add ½ cup flour which has been blended with 1 cup cold water. Cook slowly and stir until thick. Pour over chicken meat in large casserole and sprinkle with cornflake crumbs and dash of paprika. Bake in 400° oven for ½ hour. Serves 6.

Scalloped Turkey

1½ cups cooked turkey, cut in small pieces	Buttered cracker crumbs
Seasoned cracker crumbs	1 cup turkey gravy

Sprinkle bottom of buttered baking dish with seasoned cracker crumbs, add turkey meat, pour on gravy, and sprinkle with buttered cracker crumbs. Bake in hot oven (400° F.) until crumbs are brown. Serves 4-6.

Butter Baked Turkey

16-20 pound turkey	Celery leaves
1 teaspoon salt	Few sprigs parsley

OYSTER STUFFING

½ cup butter	1 pint oysters with
1 cup sliced celery	liquid
¾ cup chopped onion	2 packages (8 oz. ea.)
½ cup grated carrot	herb seasoned stuffing
Broth or water	

If turkey is frozen, thaw day before roasting. Simmer turkey neck and giblets in water to cover with salt, celery leaves and parsley until fork tender. Strain liquid; refrigerate for gravy. Remove meat from neck; chop with giblets in small pieces. Refrigerate until ready to use for stuffing. When turkey is ready to stuff, rinse body and neck cavities with cold water, Drain. Salt cavities lightly. To prepare stuffing: in medium-sized skillet, melt butter; add celery, onion and carrot, saute 5 minutes. Add oysters and liquid and simmer, stirring occasionally, until edges of oysters curl. Combine stuffing with sauteed vegetables and oysters in bowl; toss lightly. Add broth to moisten stuffing. To stuff turkey: Pack stuffing lightly in body and neck cavity. Fasten neck skin side down by folding wings back akimbo or with poultry pin. Fasten legs according to packer's directions.

Minced Turkey

1 cup cooked turkey, diced	1/3 cup soft, stale bread crumbs
Onion juice	1 cup turkey gravy

Season gravy with onion juice. Add turkey and crumbs. Heat. Serve on toast garnished with toast points. Serves 4.

Pigeon Pie

6 pigeons
Salt pork fat
½ teaspoon peppercorns
I onion stuck with 8 cloves
8 slices carrot

2 sprigs parsley
2 stalks celery
4 tablespoons butter
3 tablespoons flour

Dress, clean and truss pigeons and saute in fat until entire surface is seared, turning frequently. Put in kettle nearly cover with boiling water, and add peppercorns, onion, carrot, parsley and celery, and simmer 3 hours or until tender. Remove pigeons, strain liquor and thicken with butter and flour cooked together. Reheat pigeons in sauce and cover with pastry top or serve from casserole. Serves 6.

Venison Cutlets with Apples

I slice venison, ½ inch
thick
4 apples
Powdered sugar

Salt and pepper
Butter
12 candied cherries
1/3 cup port

Wipe, core and cut apples in ¼-inch slices. Sprinkle with powdered sugar, add wine, cover and let stand 30 minutes. Drain (reserving wine) and saute in butter. Cut venison in cutlets, sprinkle with salt and pepper, cook 3 or 4 minutes in lightly greased pan. Remove from pan. Milet 3 tablespoons butter in pan, add wine drained from apples and cherries. Reheat cutlets in sauce and serve with apples. Serves 4-6.

Sauteed Quail A La Mouquin

6 quail, dressed, cleaned
and trussed
½ cup butter
2 shallots, finely chopped
2 cloves garlic, finely
chopped
½ bay leaf
I teaspoon finely cut chives

I teaspoon peppercorns
2 cloves
I pint white wine
I pint heavy cream
½ teaspoon salt
1/8 teaspoon pepper
Few grains cayenne

Cook butter with shallots, garlic, bay leaf, peppercorns, and cloves for 8 minutes, stirring constantly. Saute quail in mixture until well browned. Add wine and simmer 30 minutes. Remove quail, strain sauce into a casserole, and add cream slowly. Add remaining seasonings and quail, cover, and heat to boiling point. Serve in casserole. Serves 6.

Chicken Tamale Pie

Line large or individual baking dishes with cooked corn meal. Lay in slices of cooked chicken. Mix stewed fresh or canned tomatoes with fresh or canned corn, season highly with minced onion, chili peppers, salt and pepper, and pour over chicken. Cover with cooked corn meal. Sprinkle with minced bacon or grated cheese. Bake in moderate oven (350° F.) until brown.

MEATS

Veal Loaf

3 Pounds upper portion leg of veal, chopped fine

¼ pound salt pork, chopped fine

2 eggs, well beaten

1 cup powdered crackers

1 teaspoon salt

1 teaspoon pepper

1 teaspoon sage

Mix ingredients together thoroughly and bake in a loaf pan for 1 hour and 15 minutes.

Pot Roast

Melt in a hot frying pan a lump of butter or fry out a small piece of pork; while very hot put in the roast, browning all sides. Rool it over; no not insert fork, so as to keep all juices in. When browned, put in a pot which has been heated; add water to frying pan to get any juices that have escaped and pour over meat. Cover and cook slowly for 3 hours, turning occasionally. Keep about 1 cup of water under the meat and sprinkle with flour and· salt 15 minutes before removing from oven, turning several times. A chopped onion added while cooking gives it a good flavor.

Ham Croquettes

¼ cup butter or margarine
¼ cup flour
½ teaspoon salt
½ teaspoon paprika

1½ cups rich milk
1 cup boiled rice
1 cup chopped ham
1 egg, beaten light

Make a sauce by melting the butter and blending in flour and salt; add the egg, cook until thicken. (Do not allow to boil). Add rice and ham (cooked, mix thoroughly and turn on a dish to cool). Form into balls or cylinder shapes, roll in soft, sifted bread crumbs then in a beaten egg diluted with 3 or 4 tablespoons of milk or water, and again in crumbs. Fry in deep fat, preferably vegetable oil.

Brown Fricassee of Veal

Melt 4 tablespoons of shortening in iron frying pan. Cut veal steak in pieces for serving; roll in flour and set to cook in the hot fat. Brown veal on both sides, then add light broth or water to cover and let cook (simmer) for 1 hour. Stir ¼ cup flour (for each pint of liquid), ½ teaspoon salt, and ¼ teaspoon pepper with cold water to form a smooth, thin paste; add to meat, stir until boiling and let simmer 10-15 minutes until served. A little tomato puree is a good addition to the sauce.

Cutlets of Lamb

1 cup cold cooked lamb
3 slices cooked bacon
3 anchovies
2 tablespoons brown sauce
½ teaspoon paprika
1 teaspoon finely chopped parsley

1 egg, beaten light
½ teaspoon salt (scant)
1 teaspoon grated onion
1 egg, 4 tablespoons milk
Soft, sifted bread crumbs
Oil for frying

Separate meat from unedible portions and put with bacon and anchovies through food chopper; add the sauce (left over with the meat) and the remaining ingredients and mix thoroughly. Form the mixture into balls and flatten into cutlet shapes; roll in flour, then in egg, beaten and mixed with milk, then in crumbs. Fry in hot vegetable oil.

Boiled Ham

Soak ham several hours overnight, after scraping and scrubbing thoroughly with a brush. To cook, cover with water, bring slowly to boiling point, let boil a few moments, then skin and let simmer 5 hours or more. When tender, set aside to partially cool in the liquid, remove from pan, draw off skin. Brush over with beaten yolk of egg, diluted with milk, sprinkle with brown sugar and cracker crumbs (mixed together) and brown in oven. Garnish dish with parsley. May be served cold in thin slices.

Sauerbraten Pot Roast

1 4-5 pounds pot roast	6 whole cloves
1 tablespoon salt	1 bay leaf
3 chopped onions	2 cups vinegar
4 lemon slices	1½ cups water
1 tablespoon sugar	2 tablespoons flour
12 whole peppercorns	Salt and pepper to taste

Rub roast with salt and put in large bowl. Mix onions, lemon, sugar, peppercorn, cloves, bay leaf, vinegar, and 1 cup of water. Bring to boiling point and pour over pot roast. Marinate roast frequently for 3 hours turning occasionally. Then transfer roast to large covered saucepan and marinate. Simmer, covered for 2 hours or until meat is tender. Remove meat to platter. Strain gravy and remove excess fat. Mix remaining cup of water and flour and stir into gravy. Cook until gravy bubbles and thickens, stirring constantly to prevent lumping. Season with salt and pepper.

Meat Loaf Supreme

1 pound ground ham	1 cup sour cream
1 pound ground pork	½ cup chopped green pepper
1 cup soft bread crumbs	1 teaspoon dry mustard
1 egg, beaten	½ teaspoon salt

In a bowl lightly mix ham, pork, bread crumbs, egg, sour cream, green pepper, mustard and salt just until blended. On a shallow baking pan shape into loaf. Bake in preheated oven 350° 1½ hours. Allow to stand 10 minutes before removing. Serves 8. Top with Horseradish Cheese Sauce (see sauces).

LUMBERJACKING

Aroostook timber built up its own distinctive universe of lumber jacks, and just as potato is king in Aroostook today, so was lumber her king 75 to 100 years ago. The beginning story of Aroostook lies primarily in the chronicle of the axe. It tells of arms strong enough and hands tough enough to weild it. Timber meant pioneering by the axe instead of the six-shooter. Lumberjacks from all over the world gathered in the Aroostook. They were strong men speaking in many tongues and brogues: all knew the universal language of the falling axe.

The lumbermen of old Aroostook cut and hauled not merely clumps and groves, but scattering trees of outstanding timber value in gay disregard of location. But a loggers life many times was far from gay. It was danger, suffering, hunger, frost bite and unexpected sudden death.

Lumberjacks worked in teams, often staying in the woods for days at a time. Campfires burned in the wilderness beside the river which floated the timber downstream to the mills. Sometimes wolf packs attacked the team, big menancing winter-starved wolves. The manual dangers of timbering proved more hazarderous however, than the over-sized timber wolves.

The axe was a lumberjacks best friend, and worst enemy. It meant felling a tree, but it also meant severed limbs. Aroostook lumbering is dead, killed off not by ravaging fires or wielded axes. Rather the lumber saga of Aroostook is finished and the abundant forests are now left to the fish, game, sportsman and nature lover to enjoy and appreciate.

Meat Balls in Sour Cream Sauce

1 pound ground beef	2 tablespoons butter
1 cup soft bread crumbs	1 can (1 lb.) tomatoes
¼ cup chopped onion	½ cup tomato liquid
1 egg, slightly beaten	2 tablespoons flour
¼ cup milk	½ cup chopped green pepper
1 teaspoon steak sauce	1 cup sour cream at room
½ teaspoon garlic salt	temperature
½ teaspoon seasoned salt	Hot buttered rice
1/8 teaspoon pepper	

In a bowl combine ground beef, bread crumbs, onion, egg, milk, steak sauce, garlic and seasoned salts and pepper just until blended. Shape into 18 meat balls. In large covered skillet melt butter; slowly brown meat balls. Drain ½ cup liquid from tomatoes. In a small bowl combine flour and tomato liquid until smooth and set aside. Add remaining tomatoes and green pepper to skillet; cover and simmer 20 minutes. Remove meat balls to warmed platter. Gradually add flour mixture to tomatoes in skillet; cook and stir until thickened. Cook 2 additional minutes. Reduce heat to very low; stir in sour cream. Heat to serving temperature. Serve over hot buttered rice. Serves 6.

Beef and Mushroom Casserole

1 pound lean beef	1 can cream of mushroom soup

Cut beef into servings. Pound flour, salt and pepper into it. Brown in skillet and place in casserole. Dilute soup ½ with water and pour over meat. Bake, covered, 1½ hours at 325° F.

Meat Loaf Ring

2 pounds ground chuck
2 eggs, beaten
1½ cups soft bread crumbs
1½ tablespoons prepared
　horseradish
1 tablespoon prepared
　mustard

1 tablespoon instant
　minced onion
½ cup milk
1 teaspoon salt
1 cup (4 oz.) Cheddar
　cheese cubes
Cheddar cheese slices

In a bowl lightly mix chuck, eggs, bread crumbs, horseradish, mustard, onion, milk and salt; then add cheese cubes. Pack into a 4½ cup ring mold; unmold onto shallow baking pan. Bake in a pre-heated 350° oven about 1 hour. Top with cheese slices; if necessary return to oven to melt cheese. Let stand 10 minutes; remove to serving platter. Fill center with whipped potatoes. Makes 6-8 servings.

Pork Pie

1 pound ground pork
1 cup mashed potatoes
1 stock celery

Salt and pepper
1 small onion
½ teaspoon poulty seasoning

Cook potatoes with stock of celery. When cooked remove celery and mash. Chop onion and fry in butter in medium hot pan, then add chopped pork and stir constantly until pork is well cooked. Add mashed potatoes and mix thoroughly and add poultry seasoning. Bake 15 minutes at 450° F. Makes 1 two-crust 9-inch pie.

Ham and Egg Pie

4 eggs, slightly beaten
¼ teaspoon pepper
¼ teaspoon baking powder
½ cup milk

2 cups cooked ham, cut
in ½-inch cubes
1 cup grated cheese

Beat eggs slightly and add pepper, baking powder, milk, ham and cheese. Pour ham mixture into unbaked pie shell. Bake in very hot oven (475° F.) 20 minutes or until knife inserted comes out clean. Serve with grilled tomatoes or green salad. Serves 6.

Lamb Casserole

3 pounds of shoulder lamb
cut in pieces for serving
2 cups sliced carrots

2 cups diced celery
1 green pepper, cut fine
2 cups onion, cut fine

Brown the lamb on all sides in hot frying pan. Place a layer in the bottom of casserole then a layer of mixed vegetables season with salt, pepper, ½ teaspoon of sweet basil, ½ teaspoon of thyme and 2 tablespoons minute tapioca. Repeat and add water to just cover. Cook 4 hours in 350° oven. Before serving, add 1 can of peas, drained.

Veal Casserole

2 pounds veal round steak cut in 1-inch square pieces

¼ pound bacon, cut in small pieces

4-6 onions, chopped fine

2 teaspoons salt

3 tablespoons paprika

1½ cups uncooked macaroni

2 cups sour cream

Brown meat, bacon and onions in saucepan, or deep skillet with 2 tablespoons butter on large unit on high, then add seasoning, macaroni and cream, high to steam. Warm to 1½ hours.

Roast Saddle of Venison with Mint Sauce

Soak meat in water overnight, then with knife take off all three skins. In taking off inner skin, begin at lower side and go upward to top of bone. Then insert small pieces of salt pork, wrap roasting piece in cloth saturated with vinegar and let stand until the next day. Put a few slices of salt port into pan, lay roast on it, salt meat well, add small amount of water, then pour over meat and half cup of cream, and baste meat frequently with juices. Bake in medium oven, as any roast of beef, until done.

Sauce: 4 tablespoons spearmint (if fresh is used, chop fine). Add 2 tablespoons sugar and add the juice from meat roast to make 1 cup. Heat and thicken as any gravy.

Smothered Round Steak

3 slices fat salt pork, 3 x 4 inches	1½ cups cold water
1 onion, cut thin slices	¼ teaspoon salt
2 pound slice round steak	1 tablespoon butter
	2 tablespoons flour

Try out pork and add onion. Cook, stirring constantly, until onion is brown. Put in water and salt. Bring quickly to boiling point, add steak cover closely, lower heat, and simmer until meat is tender. Remove steak to hot platter and strain stock, of which there should be 1 cup. Melt butter, add flour, and stir until well blended; then pour on gradually, while stirring constantly, hot stock. Bring to boiling point, season with salt and pepper, and pour over steak. Serves 6.

Chili Con Carne

1 pound beef (round or neck)	1 tablespoon chilli powder
1 tablespoon flour	1 clove garlic or
½ teaspoon salt	¼ cup chopped onion
2 tablespoons chopped suet or bacon fat	1 large can tomatoes
	1 large can kidney beans

Melt suet or bacon fat, add garlic or onion, and cook until slightly yellow. Add meat, chopped or cut in small cubes. Sprinkle with salt and flour. Stir and cook until meat is browned. Add other ingredients, cover, and simmer until meat is tender (1 hour or more). Serves 4.

Steak and Kidney Pie

1½ pounds top round steak	1¼ tablespoons
3 lamb's kidneys	Worcestershire
1½ sliced onions	2 tablespoons flour
2½ tablespoons butter	½ teaspoon salt
1 1/3 cups boiling water	1/8 teaspoon pepper

Wipe steak, remove fat, and cut lean meat in ¾-inch cubes. Soak, pare, trim, and cut kidneys in ¼-inch cubes. Fry out fat removed from steak; add onion and stir constantly till well browned. Add 1 tablespoon butter, beef, and kidneys and stir constantly until entire surface of meat is well seared and browned; then remove to stewpan. To fat remaining in pan add boiling water and strain; add Worcestershire sauce, salt, and pepper. Pour over meat, cover tightly, and let cook over low heat until meat is tender. Strain off liquid remaining in pan and thicken with remaining butter and flour mixed together. Serve as a stew or with pastry top.

Pork Steak with Pineapple

1 slice fresh pork or fresh ham 1½ inches thick	1 teaspoon salt
2 tablespoons flour	¼ teaspoon pepper
	3 slices pineapple

Put meat in casserole. Rub with flour, salt and pepper. Cut pineapple slices in half and arrange on meat. Cover. Cook 1½ hours in moderate oven (350° F.). Serves 6.

Corned or Roast Beef Hash

2 cups cooked corned or roast beef, chopped
3 cups cold boiled potatoes, chopped

Milk or cream
Salt and pepper
Onion juice or chopped onion, to taste

Combine beef and potatoes. Season and moisten with milk or cream, put into a hot buttered frying pan, stir until well mixed, spread evenly, then place over low heat where it may brown slowly underneath (40-45 minutes). Use asbestos mat if cooked on gas stove. Turn and fold on a hot platter. Garnish with sprig of parsley in the middle. Choped parsley, chopped green or red pepper, or pimientos cut in small pieces may be added to hash mixture. Serves 6.

Shepherd's Pie

½ cup diced cooked carrots
½ cup cooked peas
½ cup diced cooked turnip
1 tablespoon chopped onion
1½ cups diced cooked meat
1/3 cup diced celery

2/3 cup gravy or vegetable cream sauce
¼ teaspoon salt
1/8 teaspoon paprika
1 cup mashed potatoes
2 tablespoons cream

Mix together vegetables, meat, celery, gravy, salt and paprika. Pour into a buttered shallow baking dish. Heat potatoes and cream in double boiler. When hot beat thoroughly and spread roughly over vegetable-meat blend. Bake 25 minutes in moderate oven.

Fried Salt Pork, Country Style

½ pound salt pork	¼ teaspoon salt
Corn meal	Few grains pepper
Flour	I tablespoon butter
I cup milk	I½ cups boiled potato cubes

Cut pork in thin slices, and slices in halves crosswise (making pieces about 2 x 3 inches), and gash each rind edge 4 times. Dip in corn meal and flour. Cook in hot frying pan until crisp and well browned, turning frequently. Remove from pan. Serves 4.

Milk Gravy   Strain fat through a double thickness of cheesecloth placed over a fine strainer. Put 1½ tablespoons fat in saucepan, add 2 tablespoons flour, and stir until well blended. Add milk, gradually, while stirring constantly. Bring to boiling point and add salt and butter, bit by bit. Add cooked potato cubes to gravy. Pile in center of hot serving dish and surround with prepared pork. Garnish with sprigs of parsley.

Casserole of Ham

I slice ham, 2 inches thick	I½ cups potatoes, pared
2 cups milk	and thinly sliced

Wipe ham, remove outside edge of fat. Put in casserole, and cover with potatoes. Add milk, cover, and bake 1½-2 hours in moderate oven (350°). Serves 6 or more.

Baked Stuffed Pork Chops

4 rib pork chops, cut
　I-inch thick
I tablespoon chopped onion
¼ cup diced celery
2 tablespoons cooking oil
2 cups dry bread crumbs

½ teaspoon salt
1/8 teaspoon pepper
¼ teaspoon sage
1/8 teaspoon poultry
　seasoning
½ cup chicken broth

Slit a pocket along the rib side of each chop. Prepare the stuffing by browning the onions and celery in the oil and mixing with salt, pepper, bread crumbs, sage, poultry seasoning and broth. Stuff each chop with ¼ of mixture. Season chops with salt and pepper. Place in baking pan and bake, covered for 1 hour in 350° oven. Uncover and continue baking for 30 minutes or until brown. Remove chops from pan, add ¾ cup water and simmer for 5 minutes. Mix 1½ tablespoons corn starch with ¼ cup water. Stir into stock in baking pan. Simmer until cornstarch is cooked. Season with salt and pepper and accent. Serve with warm applesauce. Serves 4.

Boiled Round of Beef with Horseradish Sauce

5 pounds bottom round
¼ tablespoon parsley
2 oz. onions, chopped fine

¼ tablespoon salt
2 oz. carrots, chopped fine
2 oz. celery, chopped fine

Brown beef in oven at 350°. Place meat in kettle with enough water to cover and simmer 5 minutes. Use ladle and skim. Add remaining ingredients and simmer until fork can be put through thickest part.

Horseradish Sauce Mix ½ pint cream sauce and ¼ cup hot horseradish and season to taste. Grated lemon rind may be added also. Serves 8.

Swedish Meat Balls — Family Style

1 pound ground beef	1/8 teaspoon ground cloves
¼ cup finely chopped onions	1 egg
1 teaspoon salt	4 slices dried bread
¼ teaspoon pepper	Flour
¼ teaspoon allspice	2 tablespoons fat
2 cups beef consomme	2 tablespoons flour

Mix meat, onions, seasonings, and egg. Dip bread into water and squeeze dry. Crumble bread into very small pieces and add to meat mixture. Mix well and form into balls. Roll in flour and brown in hot fat. When browned, remove from skillet and pour off fat except for approximately 2 tablespoons which is added to the 2 tablespoons flour. Stir until smooth. Gradually add consomme, stirring constantly until mixture has boiled 3 minutes. Place meatballs in skillet with sauce, cover and simmer 15 minutes. Season to taste. Serves 5-7.

Braised Short Ribs of Beef

2 pounds beef shortribs cut in serving portions	1¼ cups water
	1 onion, sliced
1 teaspoon salt	1 tablespoon flour
¼ teaspoon pepper	1 tablespoon Kitchen Boquet sauce

Brown shortribs on all sides in skillet. Add salt, pepper, 1 cup water and onion. Cover tightly and simmer slowly for 2 hours. Combine flour and ¼ cup water and Kitchen Boquet. Stir into broth around meat and boil 5 minutes. Serve the gravy over ribs.

Beef Strogonoff

2 pounds round steak,
   ¼-inch thick
2 tablespoons butter or
   margarine
2 tablespoons chopped onion
2 tablespoons flour
½ teaspoon paprika

Salt and pepper
1 (8 oz.) can sliced
   broiled mushrooms,
   drained
1 pint sour cream
2 tablespoons tomato paste

Cut meat across the grain in strips the width of a pencil and about 1½ inches long. Heat meat with butter and onion in skillet until meat is no longer pink. Stir in flour and cook, stirring constantly until sauce boils and thickens. Season. Cover and cook very slowly, stirring frequently, for about 1 hour, or until meat is tender. Add remaining ingredients; heat, blend well, adjust seasoning. Serves 6.

Veal Scallopini

1 pound veal steak
1 large green pepper
1 cup flour (seasoned)
1 garlic clove
½ cup olive oil

1 cup beef consomme
½ cup white wine (Chablis)
2 cups tomatoes (seasoned)
½ cup fresh mushrooms

Heat olive oil in frying pan, add garlic cloves. Saute floured veal 12-15 minutes with pepper and mushrooms. Add beef consomme, wine, tomatoes and simmer for ½ hour. Serve over noodles or rice. Serves 4.

POTATOES

Potatoes are a food for a man. This tubar has often been called the New World's greatest contribution to menus for mortals.

Maine's Aroostook County is perhaps the most famous in the country for her potato production. It is a countryside resembling many other countrysides, yet duplicating none. One salesman spoke of Aroostook County many years ago: "Why gentlemen, dough will rise twice as fast here as it does down Bangor way, and if you leave your walking stick in the ground overnight, you'll find that in the morning it has taken root and is sprouting branches and if you let it alone it'll bear apples or plums within another year."

Aroostook is indeed a land of growth and plenty. Said one potato farmer: "here in Aroostook it's mainly all potaters. We buy land and borrow money to grow potaters then grow potaters to pay back the money and buy more land. We build big houses and sheds to store potaters in, then we got to grow a mighty lot of potaters to fill up the storages. We eat potaters, work potaters, thrive, flourish and starve on em.

Thus the Aroostook potato farmer and his rich land are without a doubt the most colorful figures in Maine's agricultural history.

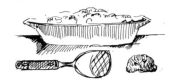

Mashed Potato Bake

2 cups mashed potatoes,
  hot or cold
2 tablespoons butter
2 eggs, well beaten

I cup top milk
Salt and pepper to taste
Nutmeg (optional)

Add butter to potatoes. (If potatoes are cold, melt the butter.) Add eggs and milk. Mix and beat well. Add salt and pepper to season. Sprinkle of nutmeg, if desired. Bake in a buttered casserole at 400° F, until well browned and thoroughly heated. Shredded cheese may be sprinkled on before baked.

Maine Baked Potato

Scrub medium size potato. Put in moderate to very hot oven 350° F. to 450° F. Potatoes take about 25 minutes longer to bake in a slow oven. At 450° F. a medium potato requires about 40 minutes of baking time. Use fork to test before taking out of oven.

Oven Browned Potatoes

6 medium potatoes

Wash and pare potatoes; boil for 10 minutes and drain. Place in pan with roasting beef or lamb. Turn potatoes two or three times. Bake about 40 minutes until tender.

Parslied Potatoes

Boiled potatoes	Few grains pepper
¼ cup butter or margarine	¼ cup chopped parsley
¼ teaspoon salt	2 tablesoons lemon juice

If "old" potatoes are used, pare, quarter, and cook in boiling salted water. If they are new potatoes, use small ones and scrape off the thin skin. Cook in boiling, salted water until tender, about 25 minutes. Drain. Add butter, salt, pepper, parsley and lemon juice. When the butter has melted, spoon some of the mixture over each serving of potatoes.

Spider Spuds

3 slices salt pork
6 medium raw potatoes

1 onion, sliced
Salt and pepper

In a heavy frying pan, fry salt pork until golden. Pare and slice raw potatoes into 1/8 inch slices. Add with onion to salt pork and fat. Season with salt and pepper. Add 1 cup of water. Cover tightly and cook slowly until potato is tender, and the water has been absorbed.

Famous Maine Potato Salad

5 medium potatoes
Garlic
1 onion, thinly sliced
2 tablespoons chopped
  parsley
French dressing

4 tablespoons chopped
  cucumber
2 tablespoons chopped
  green pepper
Salt and pepper
Mayonnaise

Boil potatoes in jackets. Peel and slice or dice into garlic-rubbed bowl. Add onion, parsley, cucumber and green pepper. Season with salt and pepper. Add French dressing and toss salad lightly. Cover and allow to chill 6-8 hours. Just before serving add desired amount of mayonnaise. Garnish with paprika. Serves 6.

Ma's Scalloped Potatoes

6 medium potatoes
3 medium onions
5 tablespoons flour
1½ teaspoons salt

¼ teaspoon pepper
5 tablespoons butter or margarine
1½-2 cups milk

Pare potatoes and onions; cut in slices 1/8 inch thick. Into a greased casserole put a layer of potatoes, then a layer of onion slices. Sprinkle with flour, salt and pepper. Dot with butter or margarine. Repeat until potatoes and onions are used. Add milk almost to top of potatoes. Cover and bake in 300° F. oven for 2 hours or until potatoes are soft throughout. Remove cover during last half hour of cooking. Serves 6.

Stuffed Maine Potatoes

3 large baked potatoes
6 frankfurters, diced
1 cup diced celery
1 small onion

2-3 tablespoons shortening
6 thin slices quick melting cheese

Saute frankfurters, celery and onion in shortening; add a little water and steam until celery is done. Allow water to evaporate. Cut baked potatoes lengthwise. Scoop out and mash potato, adding seasoning and milk until creamy and smooth. Fill potato shell with frankfurter mixture; then a thin slice of cheese and top with mashed potato. Bake in moderate oven until tops are lightly brown. Serves 6.

Bacon French Fries Bake

2 packages (9 oz.) frozen
  french fries
2 tablespoons chopped onion
2 tablespoons butter
½ pound bacon, cut into
  julienne strips
¼ pound shredded
  American cheese

3 eggs, beaten slightly
2 cups milk
1 tablespoon flour
1 teaspoon salt
½ teaspoon dry mustard
1/8 teaspoon black pepper

Brown frozen french fries and onion in butter. Arrange french fries, bacon and cheese in layers in shallow casserole using ½ of each of the ingredients at a time. Combine eggs, milk, flour, salt, mustard and pepper. Pour into casserole. Bake in 375° F. oven until mixture is set, 35-40 minutes. Serves 6.

Patio Potatoes Anna

1 (16 oz.) package
  french fries
2 tablespoons butter
Salt and pepper

1 cup shredded American
  cheese
3 tablespoons cream

Spread double thickness of aluminum foil the length required to wrap french fries. Pile ½ of potatoes on foil to one side of center. Season. Top with ½ of butter and cheese. Cover with remaining potatoes, butter and cheese. Season. Drizzle cream all over. Fold larger end of foil over potatoes, matching edges and folding over 3-4 times to make a firm package. Place on cool part of grill over glowing coals until french fries heat and cheese melts, 12-18 minutes, depending upon heat of fire. After 12 minutes open package slightly and check additional cooking time required. For indoor cooking, place package in hot (400°) oven to heat. Serves 3-4.

Skillet Potato Salad

2 tablespoons shortening
1 1-pound package frozen french fried potatoes
1 (12 oz.) can luncheon meat, cut 2 x ½ inch strips

¼ cup chopped green onions
¼ cup chopped green peppers
¼ cup French dressing
½ pound American cheese, diced

Heat shortening in skillet or frypan. Add potatoes, heat until browned. Add luncheon meat, onions and green pepper; cook until onion and green pepper are tender. Lower heat; add dressing and stir lightly. Add cheese and heat until it melts slightly. Serve immediately. Serves 4.

Boiled Potatoes

Allow 1 medium-sized potato per person or 1½ pounds new potatoes for 6. Cook a few extra to use in made-over dishes or salad. Select potatoes of uniform size. Scrub thoroughly. Pare or not (to retain full vitamin content, peel after cooking). If pared, drop into cold water to prevent discoloration. Cook in boiling, salted water to cover until soft as in pressure cooker. For 7 potatoes allow 1 tablespoon salt. Drain and keep uncovered in warm place until serving. Do not serve in covered dish. In boiling potatoes, if often happens that outside is soft while center is underdone. To finish cooking without potatoes breaking apart, add 2 cups cold water and continue cooking until they are soft in center.

Martinique Potatoes

4 baked potatoes	Salt and pepper
1½ tablespoons butter	Few gratings nutmeg
3 tablespoons cream	1 egg white, stiffly beaten
1 egg yolk, slightly beaten	

Remove inside of potatoes and force through ricer. Add butter, cream, egg yolk, and seasonings. Cook 3 minutes, stirring constantly. Add egg white gradually. Shape between 2 buttered tablespoons, place on buttered sheet, and bake until delicately browned. Serves 6.

Hashed Brown Potatoes

2 cups chopped or diced raw potatoes	Few grains pepper
3 tablespoons fat	Minced parsley, onion juice or grated onion
1 teaspoon salt	

Melt fat, add potatoes and seasonings. Cook until tender. Stir and lift from bottom, so that potatoes will not stick. Add more fat as needed. When tender, brown on bottom, turn, and fold onto serving dish like an omelet. Serves 4-6.

Potato Pancakes

3 medium raw potatoes	1 tablespoon cream
1 tablespoon flour	1 egg
1 teaspoon salt	

Grate potatoes, add other ingredients. Stir well. Cook by spoonfuls in heavy frying pan in hot fat, turning once.

French-Fried Potatoes

Wash and pare small potatoes, cut with special potato cutter or cut in eighths lengthwise. Soak 1 hour in cold water to cover. Drain. To reduce time of frying, parboil 2 minutes in boiling salted water to cover. Drain and drop into cold water. Dry between towels. Fry a few at a time in deep fat (370° F.) until delicately browned, and drain on brown paper. Heat fat to a higher temperature (395° F.), return all potatoes to fat, using frying basket, and fry until crisp and brown, keeping the basket in motion. Again drain on brown paper and sprinkle with salt. 3 cups serves 6.

Princess Potatoes

3 cups fried potato cubes
1 cup white sauce
1 teaspoon beef extract
1 tablespoon butter

½ tablespoon lemon juice
1 teaspoon finely chopped parsley

Add beef extract, lemon juice, parsley and butter, bit by bit to sauce. Add potatoes and serve at once. Serves 6.

Souffleed Potatoes

Pare potatoes and cut in even slices, 1/8 inch thick, using a vegetable slicer. Do not use end of potatoes as evenness is important for a perfect puff. Potatoes may be cut in rounds with a small biscuit cutter if slices seem large. Soak in ice water 5 minutes; drain and dry thoroughly between towels. Prepare 2 kettles of fat, one heated to 250° F., the other to 425° F. Fry potatoes, a few at a time, at the lower temperature for 3 minutes. Keep well submerged all of this time and turn at least once. At the end of the 3 minutes, lift in wire basket and put immediately into the 425° F. kettle. The potatoes will puff instantly. Continue to fry until delicately brown. Remove, drain on brown paper in a 350° F. oven until all are ready for serving. Salt and serve immediately.

Fried Potato Apples

Choose tiny new potatoes or cut large ones in shape of small crab apples. Pare, soak, parboil 2 minutes, dry, and fry like french fried potatoes. Insert clove to represent blossom end and parsley for stem and leaf. Dust with paprika. Allow 1½ pounds for 6.

Maine Potato Fritters

2 cups hot riced potatoes	Few gratings nutmeg
2 tablespoons cream	3 eggs, well beaten
2 tablespoons wine	2 egg yolks, well beaten
1 teaspoon salt	½ cup flour
Few grains cayenne	

Add cream, wine and seasonings to potato. Add eggs, place bowl containing mixture in pan of ice water, beat until cold. Add flour and mix well. To fry: Heat fat in frying kettle to 375° F. or until it is hot enough to brown an inch cube of bread in 1 minute. Dip a spoon into the fat, then take up a spoonful of the fritter mixture and carefully drop into fat, without spattering. Fritters should be cooked through and delicately brown on the outside in 3-5 minutes. Remove with skimmer and drain on crumpled soft paper.

Lyonnaise Potatoes

3 tablespoons butter
1 small onion, finely
   chopped

2 cups cold boiled
   potatoes, sliced
Salt and pepper

Cook onion in butter 5 minutes. Add potatoes, sprinkle with salt and pepper, and stir until well mixed. Cover and cook slowly until potato is brown underneath, fold and turn onto hot platter. Potatoes brown better if 2 tablespoons consomme or stock are added. Sprinkle with finely chopped parlsey, if desired. Serves 6.

Alphonso Potatoes

2 cups cold cooked
   potatoes, cubed
1 green pepper
¾ cup milk

½ teaspoon salt
1½ tablespoons grated
   Parmesan cheese

Remove seeds from pepper. Parboil pepper 6 minutes. Cut in 1/8 inch squares. Add to potato with milk and salt. Simmer 15 minutes. Put in buttered baking dish. Sprinkle with cheese. Bake 10 minutes. Serves 6.

Mashed Sweet Potatoes De Luxe

2 cups riced sweet
  potatoes
3 tablespoons butter
½ teaspoon salt

½ cup drained, crushed
  pineapple
Hot milk or orange
  juice to moisten

Mix ingredients and beat until light. Put in buttered baking dish, dot over with marshmallows. Bake in moderately hot oven (375° F.) until marshmallows melt and brown. Serves 6.

Candied Sweet Potatoes

6 medium sweet potatoes
¼ cup butter

½ cup brown sugar
¼ cup water

Boil potatoes, pare, and cut in halves lengthwise. Heat butter and brown sugar in heavy frying pan. Add potatoes, turn until brown on both sides. Add water, cover closely, reduce heat, and cook until tender and delicately brown. Potatoes may be cooked in slow oven. Serves 6.

Scalloped Sweet Potatoes and Apples

2 cups boiled sweet
  potatoes, cut in ¼ inch
  slices
½ cup brown sugar

1½ cups sour apples,
  sliced thin
4 tablespoons butter
1 teaspoon salt

Put half the potatoes in buttered baking dish, cover with half the apples, sprinkle with half the sugar, dot over with half the butter, and sprinkle with half the salt. Repeat. Bake 1 hour in moderate oven (350° F.). Serves 6.

Creamed Sweet Potatoes

2 cups cold, boiled sweet
  potatoes, cubed
2 tablespoons butter
½ teaspoon salt

1/8 teaspoon black pepper
Few grains paprika
2 tablespoons flour
1 cup top milk

Cook potatoes with butter 3 minutes. Add seasonings, sprinkle with flour, and pour on milk. Cook very slowly 20 minutes. Serves 6.

VEGETABLES

AND

SAUCES

Corn Pudding

3 cups corn
3 eggs, beaten
1½ teaspoons sugar
1 teaspoon salt
¼ teaspoon paprika

¼ teaspoon onion juice
or 1 tablespoon
minced onion
½ teaspoon celery salt
½ cup cracker crumbs
1 1/3 cups milk

Mix ingredients and pour into buttered baking dish. Set in pan of hot water. Bake in moderate (350° F.) for 45 minutes. Serve hot.

Carrot Roast

2 cups cooked rice
2 cups grated carrots
1 cup peanut butter
2 cups milk

2 eggs, beaten
1 minced onion
½ teaspoon sage
2 teaspoons salt

Mix peanut butter smooth in milk. Add rice and rest of ingredients. Bake in moderate oven (350° F.) for 1 hour.

Butter Pecan Squash Casserole

4 pounds acorn or butternut squash	½ teaspoon crushed rosemary
¼ cup butter	¼ teaspoon ground coriander
1 tablespoon grated onion	Salted pecans, coarsely chopped
1 teaspoon salt	
Butter	

Cut squash in half, remove seeds. Place cut side down in large shallow baking dish. Pour in boiling water to a depth of ¼ inch. Bake in preheated 400° oven 30-35 minutes or until tender. Reduce oven to 325°. Scoop out squash into large mixing bowl and beat until smooth. Beat in butter, onion, salt, rosemary and coriander. Turn into 1½ quart buttered casserole, sprinkle chopped pecans around edge and dot with butter. Reheat for 30 minutes. Serves 10-12.

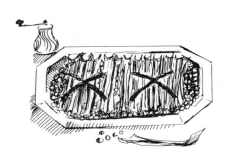

Pimiento Buttered Celery and Peas

6 tablespoons butter	2 tablespoons pimiento strips
2 cups celery, cut 1-inch pieces	¾ teaspoon salt
2 packages (10 oz.) frozen peas	¼ teaspoon onion salt
	2 tablespoons hot water

In a large covered skillet melt butter; add celery and saute 5-8 minutes. Add peas, pimiento, salt, onion salt and water. Cover and cook 4-5 minutes or until vegetables are tender. Serves 8.

Majestic Broccoli Mold

2 packages (10 oz.) frozen chopped broccoli
2 tablespoons unflavored gelatin
½ cup cold water
1 chicken bouillon cube
½ cup liquid
1½ cups milk
½ teaspoon Worcestershire
¼ teaspoon salt
2-3 drops Tabasco
1 cup dairy sour cream
3 tablespoons lemon juice
1 cup shredded Cheddar cheese
¼ cup toasted sliced almonds

Cook broccoli according to package directions; drain, reserving ½ cup cooking liquid. In a saucepan sprinkle gelatin on water to soften; add bouillon cube and reserved liquid. Place over low heat, stirring occasionally, until gelatin and bouillon cube are dissolved. Add milk, Worcestershire, salt and tabasco. Place gelatin mixture in medium bowl; chill until partially set. Meanwhile, fold lemon juice into sour cream; fold into gelatin mixture along with cheese, broccoli and almonds. Turn into 6-cup salad mold; chill until firm. Serves 8-10.

Fried Cucumbers

One large cucumber serves 3. Wipe, pare, and cut in ⅓-inch slices. Dry between towels, sprinkle with salt and pepper, dredge with flour, and saute in butter or dip in crumbs, egg and crumbs again, and fry in deep fat (390° F.). Drain on crumpled paper.

Creamed Asparagus

A 2-pound bunch serves 6. Cut off lower parts of stalks as far down as they will snap, wash, remove scales, and cut in inch pieces. Place in boiling water adding tips after first 10 minutes of cooking. Serve in white sauce or pour over a little cream, heated.

Beets, Sour Sauce

2 cups cooked beets, cubed	¼ cup vinegar
2 tablespoons butter	¼ cup cream
2 tablespoons flour	1 teaspoon sugar
½ cup water in which beets were cooked	½ teaspoon salt
	Few grains pepper

Melt butter, add flour, and pour on beet water. Add other ingredients and reheat beets in sauce. Serves 4.

Brussels Sprouts and Celery

1 quart cooked Brussels sprouts	3 tablespoons butter
1 ½ cups celery, cut in pieces	3 tablespoons flour
	1 ½ cups scalded milk

Melt butter, add celery, cook 2 minutes. Add flour and milk gradually. Bring to boiling point, add sprouts, and season. If desired, turn mixture into buttered baking dish, cover with buttered crumbs, and bake in hot oven (400° F.) until crumbs are brown. Serves 6.

Smothered Cabbage

5 cups finely chopped, raw cabbage	1 cup milk
5 tablespoons butter	2 teaspoons salt
2 tablespoons flour	¼ teaspoon pepper

Melt butter in heavy frying pan, add flour, and stir until well blended. Add milk gradually, while stirring constantly. Bring to boiling point, season, and add cabbage. Mix thoroughly, cover, and cook over very slow heat 50-60 minutes. Serves 8.

Mint Glazed Carrots with Peas

3 medium-sized carrots
½ cup butter
½ cup sugar
Butter, Salt and pepper

1 tablespoon chopped, fresh mint leaves
2 cups peas, cooked or canned

Wash, scrape, and cut carrots in ¼-inch slices, then in strips or fancy shapes. Cook 15 minutes in boiling, salted water. Drain. Cook slowly with butter, sugar and mint, until soft and glazed. Add peas. Season with butter, salt and pepper. Serves 6.

Scalloped Eggplant

1 eggplant, pared and cut in 2/3 inch cubes
2 tablespoons butter

½ onion, finely chopped
¾ tablespoon finely chopped parsley

Cook eggplant in small amount of boiling water until soft. Drain. Cook onion in butter until yellow, add parsley and eggplant. Put in buttered baking dish. Cover with buttered crumbs. Bake in moderately hot oven (375° F.) until crumbs are brown. Serves 6.

Sauteed Mushrooms

1 pound mushrooms	½ teaspoon salt
Flour for dredging	Paprika
5 tablespoons butter	2/3 cup hot water or
Dry toast	stock

One pound serves 6. Select firm, clean mushrooms, free of blemishes or soft spots. Look over carefully, brush tops, and slice crosswise. If tough, peel and reserve peel and stems for soup. Melt butter in hot, heavy frying pan. Add mushrooms, salt, and paprika. Dredge with flour and cook 5 minutes. Add water. Cook 4 minutes. Sprinkle with parsley, if desired. Serve on toast. A few drops onion juice may be added.

Glazed Onions

3 cups small, silver-	3 tablespoons butter
skinned onions	2 tablespoons sugar

Cook onions in boiling, salted water 15 minutes. Drain and dry on cheesecloth. Melt butter, add sugar and onions. Cook 20 minutes or until browned, with asbestos mat under pan. Serves 6.

Stuffed Peppers with Cheese Filling

Cut in half, lengthwise, or, if small, cut a slice from stem end of each pepper and remove seeds. Parboil peppers 2 minutes. Sprinkle with salt. Cool.

CHEESE FILLING

1½ cups grated cheese	2 tablespoons butter
1¾ cups bread crumbs	¼ teaspoon salt
1 teaspoon chopped onion	1/8 teaspoon pepper
Paprika to taste	

Put as much stuffing in each pepper as it will hold and cover top with grated cheese. Serves 6.

Baked Winter Squash with Bacon

2 pounds winter squash	2 tablespoons butter
Salt and pepper	4 strips bacon, cut in squares

Remove seeds and stringy portion from squash, bake or steam until soft, remove from shell, mash, and season with salt, pepper and butter. Put in baking dish, cover with bacon, and bake in hot oven (400° F.) until bacon is crisp. Serves 4-6.

Tomato Curry

2 tablespoons butter
½ tablespoon finely
chopped onion
1 sour apple, pared, cored
and cut in small pieces
½ cup stock

2 cups tomatoes, cut in
pieces or canned
½ tablespoon curry powder
1 teaspoon vinegar
Salt and pepper
1 cup boiled rice

Cook onion in butter until yellow. Add apple and cook 8 minutes. Add stock, tomatoes, curry, vinegar, and salt and pepper. Bring to boiling point, add rice, and cook 5 minutes. Serves 6.

Turnips En Casserole

3 cups turnips, cubed or
cut with French
vegetable cutter
¼ cup butter

1½ teaspoons salt
1½ teaspoons sugar
1/3 cup water or stock

Put turnips in baking dish with other ingredients. Cover and bake in moderate oven (350° F.) until soft. Serves 6.

Maine Baked Beans

2 pounds dry beans
½ pound salt pork
¼ cup sugar
½-2/3 cup molasses

2 teaspoons dry mustard
½ teaspoon pepper
1½ tablespoons salt
1 medium onion (optional)

Pick over beans and soak them overnight in cold water. In the morning, parboil until the skins crack when blown upon. If onion is used, cut in quarters and put in bottom of bean pot. Add the parboiled beans. Cut through the rind of the salt pork to a depth of ½ inch, and place the pork on top of the beans. Mix the sugar, molasses, mustard, pepper and salt with 1 pint of boiling water. Pour this over the beans and pork. If necessary add more water to cover. Bake at 300° F. for 6 hours or more, adding more boiling water as the beans cook.

White Sauce (Medium Thick)

2 tablespoons shortening
2 tablespoons flour

½ teaspoon salt
1 cup milk

Melt shortening. Add flour and blend smooth. Add milk gradually, stirring constantly to prevent lumping. Cook until mixture thickens. Egg yolk may be added to color mixture.

Thin Sauce: Use 1 tablespoon shortening and 1 tablespoon flour.

Thick Sauce: Use 4 tablespoons shortening and 4 tablespoons flour.

Butter Sauce for Vegetables

½ cup butter
1½ tablespoons lemon juice
½ teaspoon marjoram
¼ teaspoon salt

Dash of pepper
½ cup coarsely crushed
   soda crackers

Melt butter over medium heat, stirring constantly, until light amber color. Add lemon juice, marjoram, salt and pepper. Just before serving add crumbs. Pour over cooked cauliflower and asparagus.

Hollandaise Sauce

1 cup butter
1 tablespoon lemon juice
4 egg yolks

¼ teaspoon salt
Few grains cayenne

Divide butter into three parts. Put egg yolks, lemon juice and one of the portions of butter in top of double boiler over boiling water. Beat constantly until butter is dissolved, add second piece of butter and continue beating until butter is melted; add third piece of butter with salt and pepper and beat until sauce is of the consistency of a thick mayonnaise. Remove from heat immediately and serve at once.

Tomato Sauce

Brown one tablespoon butter with one minced onion, then add one tablespoon flour. When brown, stir in 2 cups tomatoes which have been cooked and strained. Add one teaspoon sugar, a pinch of salt, pepper and paprika. Add 1 teaspoon vinegar and 1 tablespoon tomato catsup. Serve with fish.

Hot Tartare Sauce

½ cup White Sauce
1/3 cup mayonnaise
½ shallot, finely chopped
   or ¼ tablespoon finely
   chopped onion
1 tablespoon capers
½ tablespoon parsley,
   finely chopped

½ teaspoon vinegar or
   tarragon vinegar
½ tablespoon pickles,
   finely chopped
½ tablespoon olives,
   finely chopped

To white sauce add other ingredients. Stir constantly until thoroughly heated, but do not bring to boiling point.

Raisin Sauce

½ cup brown sugar
½ tablespoon mustard
½ tablespoon flour

¼ cup seedless raisins
¼ cup vinegar
1¾ cups water

Mix dry ingredients, add raisins, vinegar and water. Cook to a syrup. Serve with ham, tongue, etc.

Mustard Sauce

2 tablespoons butter
1 teaspoon mustard
1 teaspoon Worcestershire

2 tablespoons Escoffier Sauce Diable
1 tablespoon heavy cream

Melt butter, add mustard and sauces. Stir until smooth. Add cream. Serve hot. This sauce should be of consistency of heavy cream. If it thickens too much, dilute with more cream. Serve with steak, lamb chops, etc.

Horseradish Sauce

4 tablespoons grated
  horseradish
1½ tablespoons vinegar

½ teaspoon salt
Few grains cayenne
½ cup heavy cream

Mix first 4 ingredients and add cream beaten stiff. Serve with beef.

Cold Spanish Sauce

1½ cups canned tomatoes
¼ onion
Sprig of parsley
Bit of bay leaf
  6 cloves
1/3 teaspoon salt
¼ teaspoon paprika
Few grains cayenne

3 egg yolks, slightly beaten
3 tablespoons olive oil
1 tablespoon granulated
  gelatin dissolved in ¾
  tablespoon tarragon
  vinegar and ¾ table-
  spoon cold water

Cook tomato and seasonings 15 minutes. Rub through sieve. Add olive oil to egg yolks. Combine mixtures, cook over hot water, stirring constantly. Add dissolved gelatin. Strain and cool. Serve with fish.

THE GRISTMILL

What could be tastier than home-baked bread, fresh from the oven? In olden days bread was hearth baked in ovens beside the main fireplace.

The grist for the bread was often ground in tide mills located on streams and ocean inlets. Outstanding examples of such mills still remain standing in parts of Maine today.

One-hundred years ago flour sold for 9 to 12 dollars a barrel, with a bushel of corn or oats bringing one dollar. An evident favorite and specialty was Indian meal at only 2¢ a pound. Quite a change from today's prices!

Grain was received from the farmers wagons to be ground. It was first cleaned, then ground, sifted, weighted, stamped and finally bagged or barreled.

In colonial America the sturdy gristmill was the hub of community life. Here farmers gathered to have their grain ground into flour, to exchange local news and transact business. Usually these mills were the largest structures in rural communities and going to see the miller, with his roaring machinery was an adventuresome visit for the young and an experience of never-ending interest to the old.

No wonder this crusty staple was enjoyed by all. Envision it now, a slice of hot, home-baked bread dripping with mouthwatering creamery butter!

Potato Bread

1/3 cup hot water or milk	3 cups mashed potatoes
2 teaspoons salt	½ cake compressed yeast
2 teaspoons shortening	¼ cup warm water
3 teaspoons sugar	6 cups sifted flour

Combine hot water or milk, salt, shortening and sugar in bowl, add mashed potatoes and mix well. Soften the yeast in warm water and add to the potatoes. Add 1 cup flour and knead thoroughly, then add second cup, kneading thoroughly, and remaining cups. Let rise until double its bulk (about 3 hours). Knead slightly and shape into loaves. Let rise until double its bulk and bake in moderate oven at 375° for 60 minutes. Makes 2 loaves.

Maine Brown Bread

1 cup graham flour	2 cups sour milk
1 cup white flour	1 teaspoon soda
1 cup corn meal	1 teaspoon baking powder
1 cup Barbados molasses	1 cup raisins

Sift dry ingredients together, saving a little white flour to mix with raisins. Add milk, then molasses, blending well, and raisins. Steam for 3 hours.

Banana Bread

3 large bananas
1/3 cup melted butter
1 cup sugar
1 egg, beaten
1½ cups flour

1 teaspoon soda
1 teaspoon vanilla
Pinch of salt
¾ cup chopped nuts

Mash bananas with silver fork. Add butter, egg, sugar, flour sifted with salt and soda, Vanilla and nuts. Bake 1 hour at 350°. Makes 1 loaf.

Bran Bread

1 cup bran
2 cups flour
1/3 cup brown sugar
1 teaspoon soda
2 tablespoons butter, melted

1 teaspoon baking powder
½ teaspoon salt
2 tablespoons molasses
1 egg
1 cup buttermilk

Mix ingredients, and half fill loaf pan. Let rise 15 minutes; then bake for 45 minutes in moderately slow oven.

Date and Nut Bread

I cup boiling coffee	I teaspoon soda
I cup chopped dates	I teaspoon salt
½ cup brown sugar	I cup nut meats
I tablespoon butter	I teaspoon vanilla
I egg	I teaspoon baking powder
2 cups flour	

Add soda to dates and pour hot coffee over them. Let stand while mixing other ingredients. Mix flour, salt, sugar and baking powder. Add butter and nut meats and mix thoroughly. Stir into date mixture. Add egg well beaten and vanilla. Let rise 15 minutes in pan and bake 1 hour in 350° oven.

White Bread

I yeast cake	3 tablespoons shortening
2 tablespoons sugar	I pint lukewarm milk
I teaspoon salt	

Place above ingredients in electric mixer. Add enough flour to make batter and mix for 3 minutes. Let stand for 10 minutes. With spoon beat in enough flour to form soft dough. Knead on bread board about 5 minutes. Place in well-greased bowl. Cover and let rise for 2-3 hours. Bake loaves in moderate oven 350° for 1 hour. Makes 2 small loaves and 18 rolls. Rolls require 10-12 minutes baking time.

Pecan Bread

2 cups unsifted whole wheat flour
1 cup pastry flour
¾ cup brown sugar
1 teaspoon salt

3 teaspoons baking powder
2 cups buttermilk
1 1/8 teaspoons soda
1 cup pecan nutmeats finely cut

Mix whole wheat flour, pastry flour, sugar, salt and baking powder. Add remaining ingredients. Turn into buttered bread pan, cover, and let stand 20 minutes. Bake in moderately slow oven (325°). Makes 2 small loaves.

Gingerbread

1 cup molasses
1/3 cup butter
2/3 cup boiling water or 1 cup sour milk
2 1/3 cups flour
1 teaspoon vanilla

½ teaspoon salt
1½ teaspoons soda
1 teaspoon ginger
1 teaspoon cinnamon
¼ teaspoon clove
¼ teaspoon nutmeg

Put butter and molasses in saucepan and cook until boiling point is reached. Add water or milk and dry ingredients, mixed and sifted. Beat vigorously. Fill buttered shallow pan and bake 30-40 minutes; or fill buttered muffin tins ⅔ full and bake 20-35 minutes in a moderate oven (350° F.).

Honey Bread

2 cups flour
1 teaspoon baking powder
1 teaspoon soda
1 teaspoon salt
½ teaspoon cinnamon
1 teaspoon ginger
½ cup strained honey
1 egg, slightly beaten
1 cup milk

Mix and sift dry ingredients. Add others. Beat thoroughly, 15 minutes or more if convenient. Bake in loaf or bread-stick pans in moderate oven (350° F.). Add 1 tablespoon rum to mixture, if liked. Makes 1 loaf.

Pineapple Muffins

2 cups flour
3 teaspoons baking powder
1 tablespoon sugar
½ teaspoon salt
1 egg
1 cup crushed pineapple (8 oz. can)
4 tablespoons melted shortening

Sift flour, baking powder, salt and sugar together. Beat egg and add pineapple and shortening. Add to flour mixture and stir just enough to dampen the flour. Fill muffin pan ½ full. Bake in hot oven 400° for 20-25 minutes.

Potato Muffins

4 tablespoons shortening
2 tablespoons sugar
I egg
I cup mashed potatoes

I cup milk
2 cups sifted flour
3 teaspoons baking powder
½ teaspoon salt

Cream shortening and sugar. Add well beaten egg, then potatoes. Mix thoroughly. Sift flour, baking powder and salt. Add milk and flour and beat until smooth. Bake in greased muffin tins 25-30 minutes in 350° oven. Makes 12 medium sized muffins.

Apple Muffins

2 cups flour
¼ teaspoon salt
¼ teaspoon nutmeg
I egg
I cup milk

4 teaspoons baking powder
½ teaspoon cinnamon
1/3 cup shortening
¾ cup chopped apples

Sift dry ingredients together. Cream shortening, gradually add sugar. Add egg and beat well. Add dry ingredients, add milk. Add chopped apples and stir just enough to mix. Spoon batter into greased muffin tins. Place a wedge of apple dipped into sugar on top of each muffin. Sprinkle tops with sugar and bake 20 minutes at 400°.

Blueberry Muffins

2 cups sifted flour	I egg, beaten
3 teaspoons baking powder	¾ cup milk
1/3 cup sugar	¼ cup shortening, melted
¾ teaspoon salt	I cup blueberries

Mix and sift dry ingredients. Add the egg, milk, and melted shortening mixed together. Stir only enough to mix; add the blueberries. Fill greased muffin tins ⅔ full. Bake at 425° for 20-25 minutes.

Corn Meal Muffins

½ cup yellow corn meal	½ cup sugar
1½ cup bread flour	I egg
4 teaspoons baking powder	¾ cup milk
I teaspoon salt	

Mix dry ingredients and work in egg and milk. Bake at 425° for 20-25 minutes.

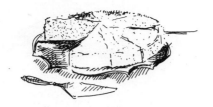

Queen Victoria Johnny Cake

2 eggs
½ cup sugar
1 cup sour milk
1 cup sweet milk

1 teaspoon soda
½ teaspoon salt
1½ cups bolted meal
½ cup flour

Mix together thoroughly and turn into a hot frying pan in which 2 tablespoons of butter have been melted. Then in the middle of the mixture turn 1 cup of sweet milk and without stirring bake in moderate oven (350°) for 30 minutes. Turn out on large plate and cut in pie-shaped pieces.

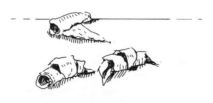

Refrigerator Rolls

1 cake Fl. yeast
2 tablespoons sugar
2 cups milk, scalded and
cooled to lukewarm

4 tablespoons melted
shortening
6 cups sifted flour
1 teaspoon salt

Dissolve yeast and sugar in lukewarm milk. Add shortening and half the flour. Beat until perfectly smooth. Add salt and remainder of flour. Knead well and place in greased bowl. Cover. Let rise until double in bulk; stir down. Cover well and place in refrigerator until needed. To use, cut off as much dough as desired, roll out slightly on floured board. Shape into rolls and place in greased pan. Let rise in warm place until double in bulk. Bake in hot oven at 425° for 20 minutes.

Tea Biscuits

2 cups flour	4 tablespoons butter
4 teaspoons baking powder	2 eggs
2 teaspoons sugar	1/3 cup cream
½ teaspoon salt	

Sift dry ingredients together. Blend in butter, add eggs, well beaten and cream. Toss on floured board, roll to ¾ of an inch in thickness. Cut in squares, brush with white of egg, sprinkle with sugar and bake in a hot oven for 15 minutes.

Cream Bread Fingers

½ cup heavy cream	1 yeast cake dissolved in
2 tablespoons sugar	¼ cup lukewarm water
¼ tablespoon salt	1¼ cups flour

Scald cream and add sugar and salt; when lukewarm, add dissolved yeast cake and flour and beat thoroughly. Turn onto slightly floured board and knead. Return to bowl, cover, let rise, toss on slightly floured board and pat the roll ¼ inch thick. Shape with lady-finger cutter, first dipped in flour, arrange on buttered cooky sheet, cover again let rise, and bake in moderately hot oven (375°). Brush over with 2 tablespoons milk, mixed with 1 tablespoon sugar, and return to oven to glaze. Makes 12.

Sweet Buns

1 cup scalded milk	½ teaspoon salt
¼ cup sugar	½ teaspoon cinnamon
2 tablespoons butter	1 or 2 eggs, well beaten
1 yeast cake dissolved in	3 cups flour
¼ cup lukewarm water	

Add butter, sugar, and salt to milk. Cool to lukewarm, add dissolved yeast cake, egg, cinnamon, and flour. Mix thoroughly, cover and let rise until light. Shape large biscuits, place in buttered pan 1 inch apart, and let rise. Brush over with beaten egg or egg yolk diluted with 1 teaspoon cold water. Bake 20 minutes in moderately hot oven (375°). Makes 24 buns.

White Corncake

¼ cup butter	1¼ cups flour
½ cup sugar	*4 tablespoons baking
1 1/3 cups milk	powder
3 egg whites	1 teaspoon salt
1¼ cups white corn meal	

*Tartrate or phosphate type. Use 3 teaspoons combination type.

Cream the butter; add sugar gradually; add milk, alternating with dry ingredients, mixed and sifted. Beat thoroughly; add egg whites beaten stiff. Bake in buttered cake pan 30 minutes in hot oven (425°).

Cream Wafers

1½ cups pastry flour
1 teaspoon salt

Heavy cream (about ½ cup)

Mix and sift flour and salt. Add cream slowly to make dough. Knead on slightly floured cloth until smooth. Pat and roll as thin as possible. Prick with fork. Shape with small round or fancy cutter and dipped in flour. Arrange on buttered cooky sheet. Bake in moderate oven (350°) until delicately browned. Makes 48 wafers.

Raised Crullers

5 tablespoons sugar
1 teaspoon salt
1 cup scalded milk
3 cups flour

2 tablespoons lard
½ yeast cake dissolved in
2 tablespoons lukewarm water

Add sugar, salt and lard to scalded milk. When lukewarm, add dissolved yeast cake and 1 cup flour. Cover, let rise until light, and add 2 cups flour. Turn on slightly floured board and knead. Cover again let rise and knead; repeat. Pat and roll ½ inch thick. Cut in strips 8 inches long and ¾ inch wide. Put on board, cover, and let rise. Twist several times and pinch ends together. Fry in deep fat. 370°. Makes 3 dozen.

Molasses Doughnuts

2 eggs	I teaspoon ginger
¼ cup melted crisco	4-6 cups flour
½ cup sugar	I teaspoon cinnamon
I cup molasses	I teaspoon nutmeg
I½ teaspoons soda	I cup buttermilk

Sift dry ingredients together. Mix sugar and crisco, add eggs and molasses, then dry ingredients and buttermilk. Roll out on floured board about ¼ inch thick. Cut with doughnut cutter. Fry in hot deep fat to a light brown on one side, then turn over and fry other side.

Plain Doughnuts

2 tablespoons spry	3½ cups flour
1/8 cup sugar	4 teaspoons baking powder
2 eggs	
I cup milk	I½ teaspoons salt
¼ teaspoon vanilla	I teaspoon mace
¼ teaspoon lemon extract	

Combine spry, sugar and eggs and blend well. Add milk and extracts and mix thoroughly. Sift flour with baking powder, salt and mace. Add to blended ingredients and mix until smooth. Fry in hot spry 375°.

Baked Sausages with Creamed Potatoes

Chop, finely, 4 cold, boiled potatoes; slightly salt them and place in deep casserole. Pour over milk or cream to come nearly to top of potatoes. Prick the casings of 1 pound of sausage, cover in frying basket into a kettle of hot cooking oil; in 1 minute remove and place over the potatoes. Pour 1 cup of medium white sauce over sausages, then top with ¾ cup cracker crumbs mixed with 3 tablespoons of melted shortening. Bake 15 minutes.

Savory Meat Balls and Onion Rings

½ pound chopped beef chuck	1/8 teaspoon celery salt
1/3 cup dried crumbs	1 tablespoon catsup
¼ cup grated raw carrots	4 tablespoons fat
½ teaspoon salt	4 slices onion
1/8 teaspoon paprika	1 tablespoon butter

Mix beef, crumbs, carrots, salt, paprika, celery salt, salt and catsup. Shape into 4 balls. Brown quickly in fat heated in frying pan. Add onion and quickly brown on both sides. Add butter and a little liquid. Cook 5 minutes.

Deluxe Barbecued Hamburgers

2 pounds ground beef
2 teaspoons salt
I large onion
½ cup catsup
I tablespoon vinegar

I tablespoon prepared mustard
I tablespoon sugar
I tablespoon Worcestershire
1/8 teaspoon chile powder

Shape ground beef into patties. Brown in small amount of hot fat. Combine sliced onions, seasonings, and remaining ingredients and pour over patties. Cover and cook over low heat 20 minutes. Serve in sauce in hot buns. Serves 10.

Creale Frankfurt Spaghetti

Chop 1 green pepper and ½ onion. Saute lightly in 3 tablespoons butter. Add 2 cups spaghetti in tomato sauce (prepared in can); then add ½ cup water. Place 1 pound of frankfurts across the top. Cover tightly and simmer 8 minutes. Serves 6.

Meat Loaf

1 pound hamburg	2 green sweet peppers
4 crackers	4 tablespoons catsup
1 egg	1 teaspoon salt
1 onion	Butter

Mix meat, cracker crumbs and egg with chopped onion, peppers, 2 tablespoons catsup, salt and shape into a loaf. Put in remaining 2 tablespoons catsup on top of the loaf and dot with butter. Bake 1 hour at 375°.

Creale Beef and Potato Puff

2 tablespoons butter	1 can condensed tomato
1 medium onion, chopped	soup
1 pound ground beef	2/3 cup condensed consomme
½ teaspoon salt	1/8 teaspoon pepper

Cook the onion in butter until soft; then add ground beef and brown. Add tomato soup, consomme and seasonings and cook together 5 minutes to blend flavor. While mixture is still hot, pour in casserole, cover with potato puff and bake 20-30 minutes at 425° until potatoes are puffed and brown.

Potato Puffs: Cook 6 medium potatoes in boiling, salted water Drain and shake over dry heat. Mash and beat well; add ⅛ cup hot milk, 1 teaspoon salt, dash of pepper, 1 tablespoon butter and 2 egg yolks. Continue beating until thoroughly mixed. Fold in 2 beaten egg whites and drop by the spoonfuls on top of meat mixture.

Liver Patties

½ pound beef liver
1 cup sifted bread crumbs
¼ cup milk
4 slices bacon

1 teaspoon grated onion
¾ teaspoon salt
Dash pepper

Chop raw liver very fine. Mix with crumbs, milk, onion, and seasonings. Shape into patties. Wrap with bacon and bake in hot oven 450° F. for 10 minutes, then reduce heat to 325° and bake 15 minutes longer.

Bologna Beef Loaf

1½ pounds chuck beef, ground
¼ pound bologna, ground
1 cup soft bread crumbs
2 eggs, well beaten
1 cup milk

1 teaspoon salt
1 teaspoon celery seed
¼ teaspoon pepper
1 tablespoon mustard
½ cup minced onions

Combine ground beef and bologna, add remaining ingredients. Turn into a greased loaf pan 10" x 5" x 3". Bake in moderate oven at 350° F. for 70 minutes. Serve hot or cold.

Sub Gum Gai Pen

2 cups raw chicken	2 cups thin-sliced celery
2 tablespoons fat	½ cup chicken bouillon
1 teaspoon salt	3 small tomatoes, peeled
1/8 teaspoon cayenne	2 tablespoons cornstarch
2 tablespoons minced	2 tablespoons soy sauce
green pepper	¼ cup cold water
1 cup thin-sliced cabbage	3 cups hot cooked rice

Use roasting chicken 4 pounds after being drawn. Remove skin from meat and cut into ⅓ inch dices, then measure. Heat fat in skillet; add chicken, salt and cayenne. Saute 10 minutes stirring occasionally. Add next 4 ingredients. Cover and cook 10 minutes. Add peeled and quartered tomatoes, then cornstarch and soy sauce, stirred smooth with cold water. Cook covered, 3-4 minutes longer, or until ingredients are thoroughly heated, stirring frequently. Serve with rice. Serves 4.

Richmond Russian Salianka

1 chopped onion	1 cup stock
¼ pound butter, flour	1 cup cubed bologna
1½ pounds sauer kraut,	½ cup chopped mushrooms
drained	½ cup chopped black olives

Fry chopped onions in butter until golden brown. Add a little flour and brown; add sauer kraut, stock, bologna, mushrooms and black olives. Heat and serve in casserole.

Chicken Chop Suey

1 cup shredded cooked chicken	1 cup chopped celery and leaves
2 tablespoons butter	1 cup bean sprouts
½ cup chopped green peppers	¾ cup chicken broth
½ cup chopped onions	2 tablespoons cornstarch
½ cup toasted almonds	2 tablespoons soy sauce

Melt butter in a skillet, add green peppers and onions and cook for a few minutes, but do not brown. Add the meat and cook 5 minutes. Add celery, bean sprouts and broth, reserving enough to make a paste with the cornstarch. Add the paste to the mixture and cook gently for 10 minutes, stirring well. Stir in toasted almonds and soy sauce. Mushrooms may be added, if desired. Serve on hot rice.

Spring Hash

3 cups mashed potatoes	2 eggs, well beaten
Salt and pepper to taste	¼ cup milk
1 can corn beef or	1 small onion, chopped fine
2 cups left-over corn beef	8 eggs

Have fresh, hot, mashed potatoes seasoned with salt and pepper. Add corn beef, crumbled up and beat together thoroughly. Add 2 beaten eggs and milk and whip until mixture is very light. Bake in casserole and serve with dropped eggs on top.

Jellied Steak Loaf

2 pounds round steak
   cut in 1-inch cubes
1 sliced onion
2 stalks celery
1 carrot
Few sprigs parsley
3 cups boiling water
1 cup canned tomato juice
1 tablespoon and ½
   teaspoon vinegar

2 ¾ teaspoons salt
1 ½ tablespoons plain
   unflavored gelatin
1/8 teaspoon pepper
¼ teaspoon dry mustard
½ teaspoon bottled, thick
   condiment sauce
1 teaspoon bottled
   horseradish

Place cubed steak in kettle with next 6 ingredients and 1 tablespoon vinegar and 2 teaspoons salt. Simmer, covered 1½ hours. Drain reserving liquid. Grind meat through medium-blade food chopper, cool ½ cup liquid. Soak gelatin in this for 5 minutes. Dissolve in remaining 3½ cups liquid heated to boiling. Add ¾ teaspoon salt, ½ teaspoon vinegar, pepper, mustard, condiment sauce and horseradish. Chill until beginning to thicken. Add meat and pour into wet loaf pan and chill until firm. Unmold on platter, garnish with lettuce and serve with horseradish cream. Serves 8.

Baked Macaroni and Cheese

2 cups elbow macaroni,
   cooked and drained
1 can (10½ oz.) Welsh
   Rarebit

¼ cup light cream
½ cup dry bread crumbs
¼ cup butter, melted

Preheat oven 350° F. Combine macaroni, Welsh Rarebit, and cream in casserole. Sprinkle top with mixture of bread crumbs and melted butter. Bake, uncovered, 20 minutes until top is browned. Serves 3-4.

Down East Beef and Potato Pie

THE FILLING:

¾ pound good beef cut in small pieces
¼ cup diced onion
1½ cups diced carrots
2½-3 cups diced potatoes

¼ cup celery, diced or a little chili powder or
½ bay leaf
Salt and pepper to taste

THE CRUST:

2 cups flour
1 teaspoon salt

2/3 cup shortening
Water to hold together

In heavy skillet melt 2 tablespoons fat and cook onion until yellow. Remove to stewing kettle. Add ¼ cup more fat to skillet and when quite warm add beef that has been dredged in well-seasoned flour. Brown, then remove to stewing kettle. Add all seasoning and water enough to stew. Cook until half done, then add potato and carrots. (If pressure cooker is used, add all ingredients together and cook at 15 pounds for 20 minutes.) When done, thicken gravy and make medium thick mixture. Cool for easier handling. Ladle out into baking bowl or individual remekins, cover with crust and bake at 425° until crust nicely browned.

Sour Cream Noodle Ring

1 cup cottage cheese
1 cup sour cream
1 egg
½ teaspoon salt
1/8 teaspoon pepper

¼ cup melted butter
¼ pound broad egg noodles, cooked and drained

Mix, fill 1-quart ring mold, well buttered, and bake 1½ hours in slow oven (300° F.). Fill as desired.

Yankee Beef Stew

1 pound boneless beef cut in 1-inch cubes	1¼ cups water
1 teaspoon salt	1 tablespoon Worcestershire
¼ teaspoon pepper	1 teaspoon kitchen boquet
½ teaspoon paprika	1 tablespoon tomato paste
¼ cup flour	4 medium potatoes, pared
2 tablespoons cooking oil	4 medium carrots, pared
	4 medium onions, peeled

Roll meat in blended salt, pepper, paprika and flour to coat each piece. Brown in 2 tablespoons oil in kettle thoroughly. Add water and seasonings. Cover tightly and simmer 2 hours. Add prepared vegetables, cover and cook for 30 minutes until tender. Note: if broth is too thin, thicken with 1 tablespoon flour mixed with ⅛ cup water and ⅛ cup burgendy and boil.

New England Baked Beans 'n' Franks

4 slices bacon	1 can baked beans
1 pound frankfurters	¾ cup barbecue sauce

In a large skillet, cook bacon until crisp, remove from skillet, crumble. Saute franks in small amount of bacon fat. Add all the ingredients and heat, stirring occassionally. Serves 5-6. Note: Home made beans may be used, if preferred.

Stew Beef with Dumplings

2 pounds stew beef
6 cups cold water
½ cup shredded carrots

1 small onion
1 teaspoon salt

DUMPLINGS:

1 cup sifted flour
1 teaspoon double acting
baking powder

½ teaspoon salt
½ cup milk

Cover meat with 6 cups cold water, heat slowly and simmer 3 hours, or until tender. About 30 minutes before serving add potatoes and carrots and stir frequently. Sift, flour, baking powder and salt together. Add milk gradually and mix to soft dough. Drop by spoonfuls on stew, cover closely and cook 10 minutes, or until dumplings are done.

Ring Around Hash Dinner

RING MOLD

2 cans (10½ oz.) corned beef hash
3 eggs, slightly beaten
1 tablespoon horseradish
¼ cup finely chopped onion
¼ cup finely chopped green pepper

CAULIFLOWER

2 packages (10 oz.) frozen cauliflower
1 cup dairy sour cream
1 can cream of mushroom soup
2 tablespoons chopped pimiento
Parsley for garnish

Combine hash, eggs, horseradish, onion and green pepper; blend thoroughly. Pack into ring mold; set in shallow pan on oven rack. Pour hot water 1 inch deep around ring. Bake 45-50 minutes. Loosen edges with spatula; turn out on serving plate. Meanwhile cook cauliflower according to package instructions. In a saucepan gently blend sour cream, soup and pimiento and heat to serving temperature. Fill center of ring with cauliflower; pour over sour cream mixture. Garnish with parsley. Serves 6.

Meat Balls in Sour Cream Sauce

1 pound ground beef	2 tablespoons butter
1 cup soft bread crumbs	1 can (1 lb.) tomatoes
¼ cup chopped onion	½ cup tomato liquid
1 egg, slightly beaten	2 tablespoons flour
¼ cup milk	½ cup chopped green
1 teaspoon steak sauce	pepper
½ teaspoon garlic salt	1 cup dairy sour cream
½ teaspoon seasoned salt	at room temperature
1/8 teaspoon pepper	Hot buttered rice

In a bowl combine ground beef, bread crumbs, onion, egg, milk, steak sauce, garlic and seasoned salts and pepper just until blended. Shape into 18 meat balls. In large covered skillet melt butter; slowly brown meat balls. Drain ½ cup liquid from tomatoes. In small bowl combine flour and tomato liquid until smooth; set aside. Add remaining tomatoes and green pepper in skillet; cover and simmer 20 minutes. Remove meat balls to warmed platter. Gradually add flour mixture to tomatoes in skillet; cook and stir until thickened. Cook 2 additional minutes. Reduce heat to very low; stir in sour cream. Heat to serving temperature. Serve meat balls with sauce over hot buttered rice or noodles. Serves 6.

Welsh Rarebit

½ pound cheese	½ teaspoon salt
½ cup cream	2 egg yolks
1 teaspoon mustard	Dash cayenne

Melt the cheese first, then pour in cream, eggs, mustard, well smoothed and seasoning all together. Heat and serve on saltines toasted.

Ham Loaf Supreme

I pound ground ham	I cup dairy sour cream
I pound ground pork	½ cup chopped green pepper
I cup soft bread crumbs	I teasoon dry mustard
I egg, beaten	½ teaspoon salt

In bowl lightly mix ham, pork, bread crumbs, egg, sour cream, green pepper, mustard and salt just until blended. On a shallow baking pan shape into loaf. Bake in preheated oven 350° for 1½ hours. Let cool for 10 minutes before placing on serving platter. Top with *Horseradish Cheese Sauce*: In a saucepan melt 2 tablespoons butter; stir in 3 tablespoons flour. Remove from heat; gradually stir in 2 cups milk. Cook over medium heat, stirring constantly, until thickened. Cook 2 additional minutes. Stir in 2 cups shredded Cheddar cheese and 1 tablespoon prepared horseradish until cheese is melted. Serves 8.

Cheese Souffle

¼ cup butter	½ pound package nippy
¼ cup enriched flour	cheese
½ teaspoon salt	4 egg yolks, well beaten
I cup milk	4 egg whites, stiffly beaten

Melt butter in double boiler; add flour and salt. Blend. Add milk and cook, stirring constantly until smooth. Add cheese, stir until melted. Add sauce to egg yolks. Carefully fold in egg whites. Bake in ungreased 1½ quart baking dish at 325° for 1 hour, 15 minutes.

COOKIES

Little Red Hen Cookies

¼ teaspoon salt	½ cup cut-up dates
2 teaspoons soda	½ cup chopped coarse
1/8 cup hot water	walnuts
1 egg	½ cup cooked, seedless
½ cup shortening	raisins
½ cup white sugar	1 teaspoon ginger
¾ cup dark molasses	1 teaspoon cinnamon
3½ cups unbleached flour	1/3 cup cold water

Dissolve soda in hot water and set aside to cool. Sift flour, spice and salt, combine with fruits and nuts. Cream shortening, add sugar and cream until fluffy, stir in unbeaten egg and mix well. Stir in molasses, add sifted dry ingredients and fruits alternately with cold water. Beat well. Add dissolved soda. Drop by spoonfuls on greased baking sheet and bake at 400° for 10 minutes. Makes 3 dozen.

Honolulu Date Squares

2 cups dates, cut fine	1 cup flour
½ cup brown sugar,	1 teaspoon soda
1 cup water	2 cups rolled oats
1 tablespoon flour	1 cup brown sugar
1 teaspoon vanilla	¾ cup melted butter

Put first 4 ingredients in saucepan and cook until thick, then add vanilla. Sift together 1 cup flour and soda, then add remaining ingredients. Spread half of flour mixture thinly on greased 8" x 12" pan. Cover with date mixture, spread other half of flour mixture and bake in moderate oven 365° for 20 minutes. Cool and cut in squares. Makes 2 dozen.

Oatmeal Raisin Cookies

¾ cup shortening
½ cup brown sugar, unpacked
2 tablespoons molasses
1 teaspoon vanilla
½ teaspoon salt
2 eggs

6 tablespoons evaporated milk
2 cups whole wheat pastry flour
2 cups oatmeal
1 cup seedless raisins
2/3 cup chopped nuts

Cream the shortening, add sugar and cream thoroughly. Add molasses, vanilla and salt and cream thoroughly. Beat in eggs, one at a time, add milk and sifted flour alternately, beating very thoroughly. Add oatmeal, raisins and nuts and blend well. Let stand to allow oatmeal to soften. Press from side of spoon on cookie sheet and bake at 350° for 15-18 minutes.

Peanut Drops

½ cup shortening
2/3 cup peanut butter
2/3 cup white sugar
2/3 cup brown sugar
2/3 teaspoon salt
1 teaspoon vanilla
2 eggs

3½ cups flour
½ teaspoon mace
1 teaspoon soda
2 tablespoons hot water
½ cup chopped roasted peanuts

Mix shortening and peanut butter until very soft. Add white and brown sugar, salt and vanilla and beat until creamy. Add eggs, flour, mace, soda, dissolved in 2 tablespoons hot water and roasted peanuts. Chill dough. Drop teaspoon full on greased baking sheet. Press top with fork dipped in flour and bake at 350° for 10 minutes.

Parsonage Macaroons

2 eggs, well beaten
1 tablespoon melted butter
1 cup sugar
Pinch salt
4 tablespoons flour
1½ teaspoons baking powder
½ cup milk
2½ cups rolled dry oats
1 teaspoon vanilla
½ teaspoon coconut flavoring

Mix ingredients and drop by spoonfuls on buttered tins about 2 inches apart. Bake in 400° F. oven until done. Add chopped nuts and sprinkle with coconut, if desired.

Blueberry Squares

2 cups flour
4 teaspoons baking powder
1/3 teaspoon salt
4 tablespoons butter
1 egg, beaten
½ cup milk
1 cup blueberries
3 tablespoons soft butter
¼ cup sugar
2 tablespoons honey

Mix flour, baking powder and salt. Cut in fat. Slowly add egg and milk. When soft dough forms, pat out on greased pan until about 1-inch thick. Cover with remainder of ingredients combined. Bake in 350° oven for 20 minutes.

Date and Walnut Kisses

2 egg whites
1 cup powdered con-
    fectioner's sugar

1 cup chopped nuts
1 cup finely chopped dates

Beat egg whites until foamy throughout. Add sugar, 2 table-spoons at a time, beating after each addition until sugar mixture stands in peaks. Fold in dates and nuts. Drop from teaspoon on heavy ungreased paper. Bake at 325° for 20 minutes or until delicately brown. Remove from paper immediately after taken from oven with sharp knife. Makes 2½ dozen.

Jam and Nut Cookie Roll

6 tablespoons butter
2/3 cup sugar
2 eggs
2½ cups flour

¼ teaspoon salt
½ cup milk
2 teaspoons vanilla

Cream butter and sugar together, add eggs, one at a time, then remainder of ingredients. Make a soft dough and add more flour, if needed. Divide in 4 parts and roll each part out thin. Spread with jam, sprinkle on coconut and finely chopped nuts. Roll in jelly roll, place rolls on cookie sheet and sprinkle with cinnamon and sugar. Bake at 350° for 30 minutes. Cut in 1-inch slices while hot.

Oatmeal Wafers

½ pound butter
1 cup brown sugar
1 teaspoon soda
¼ cup boiling water

2 cups flour
Pinch salt
2 cups Quick Quaker Oats

Cream butter and brown sugar. Add soda to boiling water, mix thoroughly in first mixture. Add remainder of ingredients and mix well. Drop by teaspoon onto baking sheet and spread out with a fork dipped in fruit or icing sugar. Bake in moderate oven 350° for 10-12 minutes.

Drop Pineapple Cookies

2/3 cup butter
1 2/3 cup sugar
2 eggs
½ cup crushed pineapple
(juice and pulp)

2 teaspoons lemon extract
1 teaspoon salt
1 teaspoon soda
3 cups flour

Mix in order given and drop on greased baking sheet. Bake at 375° F. for 12-15 minutes.

Sugar Cookies

1 cup sugar	2 teaspoons cream of tartar
½ cup margarine	1 teaspoon soda
1 egg	1 teaspoon vanilla
½ cup milk	½ teaspoon lemon extract
3½ cups flour	

Blend all ingredients well. Roll out ½ inch thick. Cut into any shape and bake at 350° for 8-10 minutes.

Mother's Brownies

¾ cup sifted flour	2 squares unsweetened
½ teaspoon baking powder	chocolate, melted
¼ teaspoon salt	2 eggs, well beaten
1/3 cup shortening	1 teaspoon vanilla
1 cup sugar	½ cup chopped nuts

Sift together flour, salt and baking powder. Add shortening to chocolate and blend. Combine sugar and eggs, add chocolate mixture, beating thoroughly. Add flour, vanilla and nuts. Bake at 350° for 20 minutes.

Brown Sugar Squares

1 cup sugar	**Mix separately for topping:**
½ cup butter	
2 eggs, well beaten	
1½ cups cake flour	1 egg white
½ teaspoon salt	1 cup brown sugar
1 teaspoon vanilla	½ cup walnut meats, chopped fine
1 teaspoon baking powder	

Mix all but last 3 ingredients well and spread in greased shallow pan 13" x 9". Beat egg whites and add brown sugar and beat until stiff. Fold in nut meats. Spread over first mixture. Bake at 370° for 25 minutes.

Fruit Nut Cookies

2 cups flour	2 tablespoons milk
½ teaspoon soda	1 teaspoon vanilla
1 teaspoon salt	½ cup chopped nuts
1 cup brown sugar	½ cup chopped dates
¾ cup butter	½ cup coconut
1 egg	

Sift together flour, soda and salt. Add sugar, butter, milk, egg and vanilla. Stir well to combine ingredients. Stir in nuts, dates and coconut. Drop by teaspoonful on greased baking sheet. Bake at 370° for 10-15 minutes. Makes 4½ dozen.

Sour Cream Sugar Cookies

½ cup butter
2/3 cup brown sugar, sifted
1 egg
1 cup thick sour cream
2¼ cups pastry flour
¼ teaspoon salt

½ teaspoon soda
1½ teaspoons baking powder
¼ teaspoon nutmeg
¼ teaspoon all spice
½ cup chopped nuts
½ cup chopped dates

Mix and sift dry ingredients. Cut in butter very fine as for pastry. Beat egg and add to cream and combine to the dry ingredients. Add nuts and dates. Drop by teaspoon on buttered baking sheet and bake at 350° for 8-10 minutes.

Honey Peanut Butter Cookies

½ cup butter
½ cup honey
½ cup brown sugar
1 egg, well beaten

½ cup peanut butter
½ teaspoon salt
2 cups flour
½ teaspoon soda

Cream butter, honey and sugar together until light and fluffy. Add well beaten egg, peanut butter and salt. Stir in flour and soda sifted together. Mix well. Form into small balls. Place on greased cookie sheet. Press with fork to flatten, passing fork both ways. Bake at 350° for 8-10 minutes. Makes 4 dozen.

Congo Bars

1 package brown sugar	½ teaspoon salt
2/3 cup melted shortening	1 cup chopped nuts
3 eggs	1 package chocolate bits
2¾ cups sifted flour	1 teaspoon vanilla
2½ teaspoons baking powder	

Put together in order given. Spread in large cookie sheet with ½ inch rim. Bake at 350° for 30 minutes. *Note*: Do not overbake. Cut while warm.

Date Bars

½ cup sifted flour	2 tablespoons soft butter
½ teaspoon baking powder	1½ cups dates, cut fine
¼ teaspoon salt	½ cup walnut meats or
2 eggs	pecans
¾ cup brown sugar	1 teaspoon vanilla

Put eggs in mixing bowl and beat until thick and creamy. Add sugar and mix thoroughly. Sift flour, baking powder and salt into creamed mixture. Add dates and nuts. Turn into well greased and floured 9" x 9" pan. Bake at 325° for 30 minutes. Cool and cut into bars. Roll in powdered sugar, if desired.

Oatmeal Chocolate Chip Cookies

½ cup shortening
½ cup brown sugar
½ cup granulated sugar
1 egg, beaten
1 tablespoon water
½ teaspoon vanilla

¾ cup sifted flour
½ teaspoon soda
½ teaspoon salt
1½ cups quick cooking oats
1¼ cups chocolate chips

Cream shortening and sugar, stir in beaten egg, water and vanilla. Add sifted dry ingredients, rolled oats and chocolate chips. Drop from teaspoon on greased cookie sheet. Bake at 375° for 12-15 minutes.

Gingerbread Men

1 cup butter
1 cup sugar
1 egg
1 cup light molasses
2 tablespoons vinegar
4½ cups all-purpose flour

1½ teaspoons baking soda
1 tablespoon ginger
1 teaspoon cinnamon
1 teaspoon ground cloves
½ teaspoon salt

In mixing bowl, cream butter; add sugar gradually and beat until light and fluffy. Beat in egg. Blend in molasses and vinegar. Sift flour, baking soda, ginger, cinnamon, cloves and salt and gradually add to cream mixture. Chill for 3 hours or more. Roll out dough to ⅛ inch thick on floured surface. Cut into any shape and place on buttered baking sheet. Bake at 375° for 6-7 minutes. Decorate or frost with Confectioners Frosting when cooled. Makes 8 dozen.

Holiday Yeast Cookies

2 packages active dry
   yeast
¼ cup warm water
2 cups butter

I cup sugar
I egg
4½ cups sifted all-
   purpose flour

Dissolve yeast in water. In large mixing bowl cream together butter and sugar until light and fluffy. Add egg and beat thoroughly. Blend in yeast. Gradually add flour. Chill for easy handling. Shape into balls 1-inch in diameter; place on buttered baking sheet. Bake at 375° for 10-12 minutes. Makes 8 dozen. Nuts or cherries may be used to decorate before baking.

Press Cookies

I cup butter
¾ cup sugar
I egg
I teaspoon almond extract

2¼ cups all-purpose
   flour
¼ teaspoon baking powder
Food coloring

In mixing bowl cream together butter and sugar until light and fluffy. Beat in egg and almond extract. Sift together flour and baking powder; gradually add to creamed mixture. Add food coloring. Shape cookies into desired shapes on baking sheets. Bake at 375° for 10-12 minutes. Decorate as desired. Makes 6-7 dozen.

Christmas Cut-Outs

3 cups sifted flour
½ teaspoon baking powder
½ teaspoon baking soda
1 cup butter
2 eggs
1 cup sugar

Frosting:
1½ cups confectioners sugar
1 tablespoon melted butter
1½ tablespoons hot water
Red and green food coloring
Colored sugar

In mixing bowl, sift together flour, baking powder and baking soda. Cut in butter until mixture looks like corn meal. Beat eggs; add sugar and beat well. Combine with flour and butter mixture. Chill dough. Roll out to ⅛ inch thickness on floured baking sheet. Bake at 375° for 6-8 minutes. Cool. To make frosting, combine sugar, butter and water; stir well. Divide in half; color one part red and other green. Using decorator tube, make design on top of cookies. Turn cookies upside down and dip into colored sugar. Makes 6 dozen.

Cherry Jewels

½ cup butter
¼ cup sugar
1 egg yolk
1 teaspoon grated lemon
   rind
1 tablespoon lemon juice
1 teaspoon vanilla

1 tablespoon orange juice
1¼ cups sifted cake flour
¾ cup finely chopped
   pecans
18 candied cherries,
   halved

Cream together butter and sugar; beat until light and fluffy. Add egg yolk, lemon rind, lemon and orange juices and vanilla; beat well. Gradually blend in flour; chill. Roll balls 1-inch in diameter; roll in nuts and place on buttered cooking sheet. Press cherry halve in center. Bake at 350° for 10-12 minutes and cool. Makes 3 dozen.

Pinwheel Cookies

½ cup butter	½ teaspoon baking powder
½ cup sugar	1/8 teaspoon salt
1 egg yolk	1 square unsweetened
3 tablespoons milk	chocolate, melted and
1½ cups sifted flour	cooled

Cream together butter and sugar until light and fluffy; add egg yolk and milk and beat thoroughly. Sift together flour, baking powder and salt; gradually add to creamed mixture. Divide dough into 2 equal parts; add chocolate to one and blend thoroughly. Chill both light and dark doughs. Roll light dough to measure 14" x 8" on floured board. Place dark dough on top of white dough and peel off paper. Roll lengthwise for jelly roll; wrap in waxed paper and chill for several hours. Cut ⅛ inch thick slices; place on buttered baking sheet and cook at 350° for 8-10 minutes and cool. Makes 5 dozen.

Orange Tea Cookies

½ cup shortening	1/3 teaspoon salt
1/3 cup sugar	1 tablespoon orange rind
1 egg yolk	1 tablespoon lemon rind
1 teaspoon vanilla	1 cup flour
1 egg white, unbeaten	

Combine shortening, sugar, egg yolk, vanilla, salt and orange and lemon rinds and cream together. Work in flour. Shape in small balls. Roll in egg white, then in chopped nuts. Flatten with spatula. Bake on greased cookie sheet at 350° for 12 minutes.

CAKES

AND

FROSTINGS

Country Cream Cake

4 tablespoons butter	½ cup milk
1 cup sugar	1½ cups pastry flour
½ teaspoon orange	2½ teaspoons baking powder
flavoring	1/8 teaspoon salt

Make a plain cake of above ingredients and bake in two layers. Remove center of one layer, moisten the edge of the other layer with egg white, and set rim from first layer on the second, forming a hollow ring. Fill hollow with following cornstarch pudding:

¼ cup corn starch	¼ teaspoon salt
½ cup cold water	2 egg yolks
1 cup scalded milk	½ teaspoon orange extract

Make meringues from two egg whites, adding 1 tablespoon of powdered sugar to each white. Drop by spoonfuls and bake on well-oiled pan in moderate oven; float on cornstarch mixture and serve cake with fresh sugared strawberries or any fresh juicy fruit.

Applesauce Cake

1 cup sugar	½ teaspoon cloves
½ cup shortening	½ teaspoon nutmeg
1 egg	1 teaspoon cinnamon
4 tablespoons hot water	1 cup raisins
1½ cups thick applesauce	½ teaspoon salt
2 cups flour	½ cup walnut meats
1 teaspoon soda	

Cream shortening and sugar. Add beaten egg and beat well. Add applesauce and hot water. Stir in raisins and nuts. Then add dry ingredients which have been sifted together. Bake in 9" x 9" x 2" pan in 350° oven for 1 hour.

Caramel Cake

2 cups sugar	½ teaspoon salt
1 cup boiling water	¾ cup shortening
3 cups sifted cake flour	1 teaspoon vanilla
4 teaspoons baking powder	2 eggs, separated

Melt ½ cup sugar in heavy pan over low flame, stirring well until liquid becomes golden brown. Remove from heat and gradually stir in boiling water, then simmer until caramel is dissolved. Sift together flour, baking powder and salt. Cream shortening until soft and smooth; gradually add remaining 1½ cups sugar. Cream until very fluffy. Beat in flavorings and well beaten egg yolks. Add flour alternately with syrup. Fold in thoroughly beaten egg whites. Bake in 2 greased layer pans at 350°-375° for 25-30 minutes.

Christmas Fruit Cake

1 cup butter	1 teaspoon soda
2 cups sugar	1 teaspoon cinnamon
1 cup molasses	1 teaspoon nutmeg
1 cup milk	1 pound raisins
3 eggs	1 cup mixed candied fruit
5 cups flour (scant)	½ cup dates
2 heaping teaspoons cream of tartar	1 cup nuts, chopped

Cream butter until light. Blend in sugar gradually. Mix in well the molasses and milk and beaten eggs. Add dry ingredients and beat well. Fold in fruit and nuts. Bake in 2 loaf pans slowly in 325° oven for 2½ hours.

Crumb Cake

2 cups flour	I teaspoon mixed spices
I cup white or brown sugar	I egg
¾ cup butter	I cup raisins
I cup sour milk	I cup chopped nuts
I teaspoon soda	

Blend flour, sugar and butter to a crumbly mixture. Put 1 cup of this mixture aside for top of cake. Mix milk, soda, spices, egg, raisins and nuts in large bowl and beat in remaining crumb mixture. Pour into greased pan 9" x 9". Sprinkle 1 cup crumbs on top and bake in 350° oven for 1 hour.

Fudge Cake with Filling

I cup sugar	I teaspoon soda dissolved in
2 tablespoons cocoa	½ cup sour milk
¼ cup butter	I ½ cups flour
I egg	¼ cup boiling water
I teaspoon salt	Vanilla

Mix ingredients in order given. Bake in shallow pan until done. When cool, split open and fill with:

I cup hot water	I tablespoon cornstrach
2/3 cup sugar	mixed with ½ cup
I tablespoon cocoa	cold water
I tablespoon butter	Few drops vanilla

Cook until thick and spread when cool.

Coconut Cake

1 cup sugar	½ teaspoon lemon extract
3 tablespoons melted butter	2 cups flour
1 egg	2 teaspoons baking powder
1 cup milk	½ teaspoon salt
½ cup coconut	

Beat together first three ingredients. Add coconut. Mix in flour, baking powder and salt alternately with milk and flavoring. Beat well for 2 minutes. Bake in loaf pan at 375° for 1 hour.

Molasses Chocolate Cake

½ cup margarine	2 tablespoons cocoa
1 cup sugar	1 cup milk
1 egg, unbeaten	2 tablespoons molasses
2 cups flour	1 teaspoon soda
1 teaspoon cinnamon	Pinch salt

Sift flour, salt, cinnamon, and cocoa; set aside. Cream margerine and sugar, add unbeaten egg and beat well. Warm the milk and molasses and add soda as pan is removed from heat. Add dry ingredients alternately with liquid to the margerine and sugar mixture. Bake in 9" x 9" x 1½" pan at 350° for 45 minutes.

Molasses Cake

1 cup sugar	½ teaspoon nutmeg
½ cup molasses	¼ teaspoon cloves
½ cup butter	2 cups flour
2 eggs, beaten	1 cup boiling water with
½ teaspoon cinnamon	1½ teaspoons soda

Cream butter and sugar. Add molasses and beaten eggs and beat until light and smooth. Add dry ingredients and beat well. Stir in boiling water until blended, then beat for 1½ minutes. Bake in 9" x 9" x 2" pan in moderate oven 350° for 45-50 minutes. Serve with hard sauce or whipped cream.

Sour Cream Gingerbread

2 cups pastry flour, sifted	1 teaspoon salt
1 teaspoon soda	1 egg
1 teaspoon ginger	1 cup dark molasses
1 teaspoon cinnamon	1 cup sour cream

Sift together soda, ginger, cinnamon and salt and set aside. Beat egg until light, add molasses and sour cream and mix well. Stir in flour, soda and spices. Beat well. Bake at 325° for 15 minutes, then raise heat to 350° until done.

Date Cake

1½ cups brown sugar	1 teaspoon cinnamon
2/3 cup shortening	½ teaspoon nutmeg
4 eggs	1 teaspoon salt
2¼ cups flour	1½ cups date (cut fine)
5 teaspoons baking powder	¾ cup milk

Mix together all ingredients except dates and beat vigorously by hand or for 2 minutes on medium speed of mixer. Add dates. Bake in 13" x 9" x 2" pan for 50 minutes or until top springs back on touch in 350° oven. Use a brown sugar icing.

Spiced Raisin Cake

1 cup seeded raisins	¼ teaspoon allspice
1½ cups water	¼ teaspoon salt
½ cup shortening	1 egg, beaten
1 cup brown sugar	1¾ cups flour
1 teaspoon cinnamon	1 teaspoon soda
¼ teaspoon nutmeg	

Cook raisins and water together for 10 minutes. Remove from heat and place raisins and ¾ cup of liquid in a bowl. Add shortening, sugar, spices and salt. Mix thoroughly. Cool slightly and stir in beaten egg, flour and soda. Pour into greased loaf pan and bake at 350° for 50-60 minutes.

White Cake

2 cups sifted flour
2 teaspoons baking powder
¼ teaspoon salt
½ cup shortening
1¼ cups sugar

¾ cup milk
1 teaspoon vanilla extract
½ teaspoon lemon extract
3 egg whites

Sift flour before measuring. Cream shortening, add sugar gradually and cream until light. Add flour, baking powder and salt which have been sifted together, alternately with milk. Beat well after each addition of flour. Add flavorings and mix well. Fold in egg whites, beaten stiff. Bake in 2 greased layer pans at 375° for 20-25 minutes.

Prize Sponge Cake

3 eggs
1 cup sugar
3 teaspoons warm water
Pinch salt

2 teaspoons vinegar
1 cup flour
2 teaspoons baking powder

Beat eggs separately. To the yolks add sugar, water, salt and vinegar. Mix well. Fold in whites. Fold in flour and baking powder which have been sifted together. Bake in muffin tins in moderate oven for 20 minutes or until a delicate brown.

Fruit Salad Cake

1 cup brown or white sugar	½ teaspoon salt
¼ cup soft butter	1 pound can fruit cocktail,
2 eggs	not drained
2 cups white flour	2/3 cup semi-sweet
¼ cup whole wheat flour	chocolate pieces
2 teaspoons soda	½ cup chopped nuts

Grease and flour bottom of 13" x 9" pan. In large mixing bowl combine all ingredients except chocolate bits and nuts. Beat 2 minutes on medium speed after ingredients have been blended on low speed. Pour into pan and cover with topping made from ½ cup brown sugar, ½ cup chopped nuts and ⅔ cup chocolate bits. Bake in 350° oven for 35-40 minutes.

Chocolate Cake

1½ cups sugar	2½ cups flour
½ cup shortening	½ teaspoon salt
1 cup sour milk	½ cup cocoa mixed with
2 teaspoons soda dissolved	½ cup boiling water
in the sour milk	2 teaspoons vanilla

Cream shortening and sugar together. Add flour and salt alternately with the soda and sour milk. Add vanilla. Stir in boiling water and cocoa which have been blended together and beat vigorously for 2 minutes. Bake in layer pans until done. Cover with favorite frosting.

Twin Elm Date Cake

½ cup soft butter	3 teaspoons baking powder
1 1/3 cups brown sugar	½ teaspoon cinnamon
2 eggs	½ teaspoon nutmeg
½ cup milk	½ teaspoon cloves
1¾ cups flour	½ pound dates, cut in
½ teaspoon salt	pieces (1 cup)

Blend all together at once. Beat 3 minutes. Pour into 9" x 10" pan and bake at 350° for 45 minutes. Top with following icing:

5 tablespoons brown sugar	2 tablespoons butter
5 tablespoons evaporated milk	

Boil 4 minutes and spread on cake. Sprinkle with nuts or coconut.

Buttercup Cake

½ cup butter	½ teaspoon soda
1½ cups sugar	1 cup buttermilk
2 eggs	1 teaspoon vanilla
2¼ cups flour	¼ teaspoon lemon extract
1 teaspoon baking powder	¼ teaspoon almond extract

Sift and measure flour, baking powder and soda together. Mix butter, sugar and eggs in bowl and beat on medium speed until well blended. Add buttermilk, flour mixture and blend with sugar and butter mixture on low speed until flour has been blended well. Add flavorings and beat 2 minutes at medium speed. Pour into well greased 2 8" layer pans and bake at 350° for 30-35 minutes. Spread favorite jam or jelly between layers and on top and sprinkle with flaked coconut.

Rhubarb Pot Shortcake

2 tablespoons butter
I cup sugar

3 cups diced rhubarb
I tablespoon flour

Melt butter in heavy skillet. Mix sugar and flour and add rhubarb. Let heat over low flame while mixing crust.

CRUST:

I ½ cups flour
1/3 cup sugar
2 tablespoons baking
powder

1/3 cup butter
I egg, well beaten
I cup milk

Sift flour, sugar, baking powder together. Blend in butter, add milk and beaten egg; mix lightly. Put this dough over rhubarb in skillet and place in 350° oven and bake 30 minutes or until crust is brown. Serve hot.

Never Fail Chocolate Cake

3 cups flour
2 cups sugar
2 teaspoons soda
2 teaspoons salt
2 cups warm water

8 tablespoons cocoa
2 teaspoons vanilla
2 tablespoons vinegar
¾ cup oil
2 eggs, if desired

Mix all ingredients together and place in greased tube pan. Bake at 300° for 1 hour.

Maple Icing

1 ¾ cups maple syrup   1 egg white
¼ cup granulated sugar

Boil the sugar and syrup together until heavy thread is formed when a spoon is dipped in the syrup and lifted or to 244° F. Then pour in fine stream on the beaten egg white, beating the white as the syrup is poured in. Set bowl with mixture on dish of hot water, and beat thoroughly until egg stiffens, then spread on cake. Vanilla may be added, if desired.

Mocha Frosting

1 cup powdered sugar   2 tablespoons coffee
2 teaspoons cocoa   ½ teaspoon vanilla
1 tablespoon butter

Cream butter with sugar and cocoa. Add coffee and vanilla. Beat well until smooth. Spread with knife dipped in hot water.

Butter Frosting

½ cup butter
6 cups sifted
  confectioners sugar
1/3 cup cream

½ teaspoon vanilla extract
3 squares bitter chocolate,
  melted
Pecans

Cream butter and gradually add sugar, thinning with cream when mixture becomes too thick to beat. Add enough cream to make a good spreading consistency. Remove about ¼ of frosting and to that add vanilla. To remaining frosting add melted chocolate. Frost half the cake with vanilla frosting and half with chocolate. Separate two frostings with double row of whole pecans.

Quick Frosting

1 cup sugar
1 egg white

¼ cup water

Cook together in top of double boiler over rapidly boiling water. Beat constantly until it stands in peaks. Add vanilla. Spread on cakes or cupcakes.

Chocolate Frosting

2 tablespoons hot cream
1 tablespoon butter
1 square chocolate, melted

1 teaspoon vanilla
1 cup confectioner's sugar

Mix ingredients. Beat well and when soft and creamy, spread over top of cake.

Lemon Frosting

2¾ cups confectioner's sugar
½ teaspoon salt
1 egg
2 tablespoons lemon juice

1 tablespoon light corn syrup
½ cup butter
1 teaspoon vanilla
1 tablespoon grated lemon peel

Mix confectioner's sugar, salt and egg. Blend in syrup, add the shortening, vanilla, lemon juice and peel. Mix until creamy. Add more sugar to thicken or water to thin frosting, if required.

Coconut Cream Icing

1 cup coconut
2 cups confectioner's sugar

4 tablespoons heavy cream
½ teaspoon vanilla

Put sugar in a bowl. Add cream, a little at a time, and beat steadily. Add vanilla. When icing is the right consistency spread over top of layers and sprinkle heavily with coconut. Put layers together and ice sides, covering with coconut.

Fudge Icing

2 squares chocolate or
2 tablespoons cocoa
2/3 cup cold milk
2 cups sugar
1 teaspoon vanilla

Dash salt
2 tablespoons dark corn
syrup
2 tablespoons melted butter

Add chocolate to milk and place over low flame. Cook until mixture is smooth and blended well, stirring constantly. Add sugar, salt and corn syrup, stirring until sugar is dissolved and mixture boils. Continue cooking without stirring until a small amount of mixture forms a very soft ball in cold water. Remove from fire. Add butter and vanilla. Cool to lukewarm. Beat until right consistency to spread.

Tart Lemon Cream Frosting

4 tablespoons butter
1 teaspoon grated lemon
  rind

3 cups sifted con-
  fectioner's sugar
3 tablespoons lemon juice

Cream butter, add lemon rind and blend well. Gradually add confectioner's sugar, alternately with lemon juice, beating until smooth. Orange juice may be substituted.

Seven Minute Frosting

5 tablespoons cold water
Few grains salt
1½ teaspoons white corn
  syrup

2 unbeaten egg whites
1 teaspoon flavoring
1½ cups sugar

It top of double boiler combine all ingredients. Beat with egg beater until well mixed and blended. May use food coloring at last minute. Place over rapidly boiling water and continue beating constantly for exactly 7 minutes. Frosting should stand in peaks.

BLUEBERRIES: FACTS AND FANCY

Blueberry pie, blueberry cobbler, preserves, muffins are just some of the tasty dishes that can be made with this succulent berry. The first blueberries were canned "Down East" in Washington County 20 years or more before they were canned commercially elsewhere in these United States. In fact, until recent years, this single county led all other states except Maine in blueberry processing.

Blueberries fall into 4 easily identifiable groups for the layman — high bush, lowbush, cultivated and "wild." Maine's broad blueberry belt extends along the coast from the St. Croix River on the Canadian boundary to the Kennebec and beyond. These berries are a low bush, "wild" type, meaning only that they do not readily adjust to cultivation.

A vast, desolate treeless tract of land called the "barrens" was where the blueberry industry got its beginnings. This tasty fruit was one of the favorite foods of the Indians who used to dry the berries in the sun and sell them by the bushelful to the English.

The blueberry industry has come a long way from the primitive days of picking berries by hand, cooked in great open kettles personally packed into hand-made cans and capped by hand. Today most berries are grown in Washington County, and the "barrens" no longer means a chief supplier of the fruit.

The next time you take a can of blueberries off the shelf, check the label. Very likely you'll find they're Maine blueberries. And let's see, what shall we make, hot blueberry pie, crusty blueberry bread, savory blueberry muffins? The list is endless. Happy Cooking!

Cherry Pie

2¼ cups all-purpose flour	4 cups canned pitted
1 teaspoon salt	red sour cherries
¾ cups shortening	1 1/3 cups sugar
Ice water	3 tablespoons cornstarch

To make pastry, sift flour and salt together, then cut in shortening with pastry blender. Add just enough ice water to hold particles together. Mix lightly with a knife, chill pastry. Meanwhile, drain juice from cherries and mix with sugar and cornstarch which has been combined. Bring to a boil over low heat while stirring; remove from heat. Line a 9" pie plate with pastry. Put in cherries and pour juice mixture over them. Roll remaining pastry to ⅛ inch thickness. Bake at 350° F. for 30 minutes.

Blush Apple Pie

5 large apples	½ cup sugar
1 cup pineapple chunks	2 tablespoons flour
2 tablespoons red cinnamon candy	1/8 teaspoon salt
1 teaspoon grated lemon rind	2 tablespoons shortening

Peel and slice apples. Add pineapple, cinnamon candies, and all dry ingredients. Mix thoroughly. Line deep pie plate with crust. Brush over bottom with part of shortening to prevent soaking. Fill with apple mixture. Dot over the apples wih remaining shortening. Cover with slashed whole crust or criss-cross pastry. Bake at 450° for 10 minutes. Reduce heat to 350° and bake 25 minutes longer.

Lemon Sponge Pie

1 cup sugar
2 tablespoons butter
2 eggs, separated
2 tablespoons flour

Grated rind and juice
of 1 lemon
1 cup milk

Cream butter, sugar and flour. Separate the whites and yolks of eggs. Beat the yolks and add to the sugar mixture. Add grated lemon, and then the milk and lemon juice. Fold in beaten egg whites. Bake with one crust for 45-50 minutes at 375° F.

Cranberry Pie

1 cup cranberries, chopped
   fine
1 cup chopped raisins
1 cup sugar

1 tablespoon flour
½ cup boiling water,
   scant
Salt and vanilla

Mix flour and sugar, add water, then raisins. Beat smooth and add cranberries last. Bake between two crusts for 45-50 minutes at 350° F.

Mincemeat Roll

2 cups flour	I egg or 2 egg yolks
3 teaspoons baking powder	4 tablespoons butter
1/3 teaspoon salt	2/3 cup milk
I tablespoon sugar	I cup cooked mincemeat

Mix flour, baking powder, salt and sugar. Cut in butter and add egg and milk. When soft dough forms, pat out until ½ inch thick. Spread with mincemeat and roll. Bake in greased loaf pan for 35 minutes at 375° F.

Mock Mince Pie

I cup molasses	½ cup butter
I cup suar	½ cup vinegar

Boil together for 1 minute. Add 4 crackers rolled, 2 beaten eggs, spice to suit the taste and 1 cup chopped raisins. Bake between 2 crusts for 50 minutes at 350° F.

All-Bran Cherry Tart

1 cup flour	½ cup chopped nut meats
1 teaspoon soda	2½ cups sour canned
1 teaspoon cinnamon	cherries
1¼ cups sugar	1 egg
½ teaspoon salt	1 tablespoon melted butter
½ cup All-bran	

Sift together flour, soda, cinnamon, sugar and salt. Add all-bran and nut meats. Drain cherries, reserving juice for sauce. Beat egg well; add cherries, egg and butter to dry ingredients. Pour into greased baking pan. Bake in 350° oven for 45 minutes. Cut into squares. Serve with following sauce: Combine 1 tablespoon cornstarch, ½ cup sugar and ½ teaspoon salt. Stir into leftover 1 cup juice from cherries, add 1 tablespoon butter and cook, stirring constantly until mixture is clear. Whip 1 cup cream until stiff. Top squares with sauce and whipped cream.

Butterscotch Pie

1 cup brown sugar	3 tablespoons cold water
3½ tablespoons flour	2 egg yolks
Pinch salt	1 cup milk

Mix in order given and cook until thick. When slightly cooled, add butter-size of egg and 1 teaspoon vanilla. Beat. Put into shell. Use white of eggs for meringue.

Sour Cream Pie

1 unbaked pie shell	¼ cup lemon juice
2/3 cup brown sugar	1 teaspoon grated
¼ cup flour	lemon rind
1/8 teaspoon salt	1 1/3 cups sour cream
1 teaspoon cinnamon	½ cup chopped raisins
¼ teaspoon cloves	1/3 cup nuts
¼ teaspoon nutmeg	3 egg yolks
1 teaspoon vanilla	

Mix dry ingredients, grate the lemon. Add egg yolks with lemon juice. Stir in nuts and raisins. Add sour cream and pour into pie shell. Bake for 10 minutes at 400° F. Reduce oven to 325° and bake 30 minutes longer. Cover with meringue by the egg whites until stiff and stand in peaks. Beat in 4 tablespoons sugar, one at a time. Spread over pie and bake at 425° F. for 8-10 minutes or until medium brown.

Pecan Pie

3 eggs	1 teaspoon vanilla
½ cup sugar	¼ cup butter melted
1 cup corn syrup, dark	1 cup pecan halves
1/8 teaspoon salt	

Beat the eggs, add sugar, syrup, salt, vanilla and butter. Line pie plate with pastry. Put in pecans in a layer and pour mixture over them. Bake at 350° F. for 50-60 minutes. Nuts will rise to top.

Pumpkin Pie

2 cups pumpkin, put
   through sieve
3 eggs
1 cup sugar
½ teaspoon cinnamon

½ teaspoon nutmeg
½ teaspoon ginger
½ teaspoon salt
1 quart milk with a little
   cream added

Mix above ingredients and pour into a 9-inch pie plate lined with unbaked pie shell. Bake at 425° F. for 15 minutes to set the crust, then reduce heat to 350° F. and bake 45 minutes longer or until a knife inserted comes out clean.

Pumpkin Pecan Pie

1½ cups mashed pumpkin
1 cup brown sugar
1 teaspoon cinnamon
½ teaspoon ginger
½ teaspoon allspice

½ teaspoon salt
2 eggs
½ cup orange juice
Grated rind of 1 orange
½ cup pecans

Mix dry ingredients, add pumpkin, milk, orange juice, grated rind and beaten eggs. Pour into unbaked pie shell and bake at 400° F. for 15 minutes to set the crust. Reduce heat to 350° F. and bake 30 minutes longer.

Raisin Pie

1 cup chopped raisins
1 egg, beaten light
¾ cup sugar
½ cup cold water

1 cracker, rolled fine
1 teaspoon lemon extract
Pinch salt

Mix thoroughly all ingredients together. Put in unbaked pie shell and cover with top crust. Bake at 375° F. for 30-35 minutes.

Cream Puffs

1 cup water
½ cup butter
1 cup sifted flour

1/8 teaspoon salt
4 eggs

Heat water and butter to boiling point in saucepan. Stir in flour all at once. Stir vigorously over low heat, until it forms a large ball in center of dish. Remove from heat and beat the eggs in, one at a time. Beat until the mixture is smooth and velvety. Drop from tablespoon onto ungreased pan about 3 inches apart. Bake at 400° F. for 45-50 minutes until puffed golden brown and dry. Cool. Cut off tops with sharp knife. Fill with whipped cream.

Tarts

3 cups flour
½ cup butter
½ cup shortening
1 teaspoon cream of tartar

½ teaspoon soda
½ cup cold water
1 egg white, beaten stiff

Mix ingredients well together. Roll out onto floured board and cut into round solid pieces. Fill cookie sheet, keeping about 2 inches apart. Cut same amount as for doughnuts and place over solid rounds. Bake in quick oven at 400° F. until brown. Fill centers with any jam, jelly or preserve.

Lemon-Apple Pie

Core, pare and chop fine 1 large tart apple. Add grated rind and juice of 2 lemons. Crush 1 cracker very fine. Melt 2 teaspoons butter and mix with cracker crumbs. Stir into the apple-lemon mixture 2 cups sugar. Beat yolks of 2 eggs to thick froth, and the whites beat until stiff, then beat both together. Mix well with the apples. Mix in buttered crumbs. Cover pie plates, putting a broad brim around the edges and fill as tarts with the mixture. Bake 20 minutes or until crust is done.

Cranberry and Raisin Tart

2 cups cranberries	½ cup cracker crumbs
½ cup seeded raisins	1 egg
1 cup sugar	Pastry
1 tablespoon orange juice	

Add ½ cup water to the cranberries and raisins; simmer gently until cranberries pop open. Sweeten, cook, add orange juice, crumbs and egg and turn into a pie plate lined with pastry. Finish the top with criss-cross strips of pastry. Bake at 375° F for 30 minutes.

Fruit Turnovers

Shape any kind of pastry into rounds of size desired. Put 1 tablespoon chopped raw and sweetened fruit, or cooked sweetened fruit on ½ of each round, moisten the edges with cold water, fold over and press together with the fingers or a fork. Brush over with milk and bake at 375° F. for 20-30 minutes.

Squash Pie

2 cups sifted squash
1 cup sugar
1 teaspoon salt
1 teaspoon cinnamon

¼ teaspoon ginger
3 cups scalded milk
2 eggs

Add the seasonings to the squash, beating thoroughly. Combine the milk and eggs, slightly beaten, add slowly to first mixture and pour in deep pie plate lined with crust. Bake at 425° F. for 15 minutes, then reduce heat to 350° F. and bake for 50 minutes longer.

Cocoanut Custard Pie

2 cups milk
3 eggs
½ cup sugar
3 tablespoons powdered sugar

1 teaspoon melted butter
4 tablespoons shredded cocoanut
½ teaspoon vanilla

Separate the eggs, beat the yolks with the sugar, butter and vanilla and add the milk and cocoanut. Line a deep pie plate with pastry; pour in the mixture and bake at 375° F. When almost done, pile on the top a meringue made of the egg whites and powdered sugar, and bake 10 minutes longer.

Cream Cheese Turnovers

¼ pound butter	1½ cups pastry flour
¼ pound cream cheese	Tart jelly or jam

Work butter and cream cheese into flour with finger tips, two knives or pastry mixer. Chill. Roll out, cut in 2-inch squares, put spoonful of tart jam or jelly on each, moisten edges with cold water, and press together to make triangles or oblongs. Prick with fork and bake in hot oven 450° F.

Sweet Potato Pie

1½ cups boiled, mashed sweet potatoes	Sugar to taste
1 egg, beaten	Salt
1 cup milk	2 tablespoons butter

Mix in order given. Bake in 1 crust in 450° F. oven until lightly brown. Flavor with rum, if liked.

Strawberry Chiffon Pie

1½ cups strawberries	½ cup boiling water
¾ cup sugar	1 tablespoon lemon juice
1 tablespoon gelatin	2 egg whites
¼ cup cold water	1/8 teaspoon salt

Wash, hull, and slice berries, cover with sugar and let stand ½ hour. Sprinkle gelatin over cold water, let stand 5 minutes, add boiling water and lemon juice, stir, and strain over berries. Stir well and chill until mixture begins to thicken. Fold in egg whites and salt, beaten until stiff but not dry. Pour into baked pie shell. Garnish with whipped cream and few perfect berries.

Lemon Chiffon Pie

1 tablespoon gelatin	½ cup lemon juice
¼ cup cold water	1 teaspoon grated
4 egg yolks	lemon rind
1 cup sugar	4 egg whites
½ teaspoon salt	

Sprinkle gelatin over cold water. Beat yolks, add ½ cup sugar, salt and lemon juice and rind. Cook and stir in double boiler until thick. Add gelatin and stir until it dissolves. Cool. When beginning to set, fold in egg whites beaten stiff with remaining sugar. Pour into baked pie shell. Chill. If desired fold ½ to 1 cup heavy cream, whipped into mixture or spread finished pie with whipped cream.

Rhubarb Pie

1½ cups rhubarb	I egg
7/8 cup sugar	2 tablespoons flour

Cut stalks of rhubard in ½ inch pieces before measuring. Mix sugar, flour and egg; add to rhubarb and bake between crusts or in 1 crust with lattice strips of pastry across top at 350° for 40 minutes.

Chocolate Cream Pie

2½ squares chocolate	½ teaspoon salt
2½ cups cold milk	4 egg yolks, slightly beaten
4 tablespoons flour	2 tablespoons butter
I cup sugar	2 teaspoons vanilla

Scald milk with chocolate. Beat until muxture is smooth. Combine flour, sugar and salt. Add to egg yolks. Pour small amount of chocolate mixture over egg mixture stirring vigorously. Return to double boiler and cook until thickened, stirring constantly. Add butter and vanilla. Cool. Pour into baked pie shell and cook at 350° for 40 minutes. Cover with meringue or whipped cream.

CANDIES

Century-Old Butterscotch Candy

1½ cups sugar	5 tablespoons vinegar
2 tablespoons butter	2 tablespoons water
5 tablespoons molasses	

Combine ingredients and boil 20 minutes, try, and if brittle pour into buttered pan or drop from teaspoon on buttered paper. Add walnut half on each wafer, if desired.

Molasses Taffy

1 cup molasses	Few grains soda
1 cup sugar	Any desired flavoring
1 teaspoon vinegar	Cocoanut or peanuts
2 tablespoons butter	

Boil the molasses, sugar and vinegar together until it "rattles against the cup" when tried in cold water (290° F.). Add the flavoring and soda and pour into buttered pans to about ⅛ inch in thickness. Bottom of pan may be covered with shelled peanuts or shredded cocoanut, if desired. When cold, mark into squares.

Popcorn Balls

Prepare molasses taffy and omit cocoanut or peanuts. Stir into 4 quarts of popped corn, then shape into balls.

Cocoanut Pralines

    2 cups light brown sugar   ½ teaspoon vanilla
    ¾ cup milk   ¾ cup shredded cocoanut
1/8 teaspoon cream of tartar

Mix sugar, milk and cream of tartar together. Bring to boiling point, then cook without stirring until a little ball forms in cold water (238° F.). Cool with tepid, add vanilla and cocoanut and beat until creamy. Drop in rounds on oiled paper with teaspoon.

Sesquicentennial Chocolate Fudge

1 cup sugar
½ cup cream
Butter size of walnut

2 squares chocolate
1 teaspoon vanilla

Mix and boil 10 minutes. Beat until thick and flavor with vanilla.

Brown Sugar and Peanut Butter Fudge

3 cups sugar
1 cup milk
1 tablespoon butter

2 tablespoons peanut butter
1 teaspoon vanilla

Cook the sugar and milk together until it forms a soft ball in cold water. Add peanut butter, butter and vanilla and beat until smooth and starts to harden. Put in greased pan to cool.

Chocolate Cornflake Candy

1 package (7 oz.)
  chocolate bits
3 tablespoons peanut butter

1 teaspoon vanilla
3-3½ cups cornflakes

Melt chocolate bits and peanut butter together in double boiler, add vanilla. Pour over cornflakes, crushed with fingers, not rolling pin. Add nuts, if desired. Drop by teaspoon on waxed paper to cool.

Fruit Chocolate Dots

Grind 1 pound each of prunes, dates, figs, seedless raisins and nut meats. Thoroughly mix together the fruit and add broken nut meats. Put into any shape mold and set aside for 24 hours. Then dip into melted dots chocolate. Place on waxed paper to cool.

Molasses Candy

1 cup sugar	3 tablespoons vinegar
½ cup molasses	Butter size of egg

Boil ingredients together until it hardens when dropped in cold water. Take from fire and stir in 1 teaspoon soda. Pour into buttered pan to cool. Nuts may be added, if desired. Candy may be pulled when cool enough and cut.

Chocolate Fudge

2 cups sugar	½ cup milk
2 tablespoons rounded cocoa	¼ teaspoon salt
	1 teaspoon vanilla
¼ cup Karo	Butter size of walnut

Mix in sauce pan and boil 3 minutes. Take off and put in walnut and vanilla. Beat until stiff. Put in pan and cool.

Uncooked Fudge

7 oz. sweet chocolate,
   melted
1 tablespoon butter
1 cup confectioner's sugar

2 eggs
1½ teaspoon vanilla
1 cup chopped walnut or
   pecan meats

Melt together butter and chocolate; stir in confectioner's sugar
and egg yolks, beaten, then the egg whites, whipped stiff. Add
vanilla and nut meats. Press into well-buttered pan, let stand until
almost stiff and cut in squares.

White Cocoanut Fudge

2 cups sugar
1 tablespoon butter
1 teaspoon vanilla
½ cup milk

¾ cup shredded cocoanut
1/8 teaspoon cream of
   tartar

Boil the sugar, milk, cream of tartar and butter together until
it forms a ball in cold water (238° F.). Remove from heat and cool
slightly; add vanilla and cocoanut and beat until creamy. Pour into
well-buttered pans, mark into squares, and cool.

Fair Fudge

2 cups brown sugar
2 squares chocolate
(1 oz.)

2 cups sugar
1 cup milk
1 teaspoon vanilla

Mix ingredients, except vanilla, together in large pan and boil without stirring until a ball forms in cold water (238° F). Cool until it can be dented, add vanilla and beat until creamy.

Marshmallow Fudge

2 cups light brown sugar
½ cup milk
1 cup marshmallows,
cut in quarters

1 teaspoon butter
½ teaspoon vanilla
1/8 teaspoon cream of
tartar

Cook sugar, cream of tartar and milk without stirring until a ball forms in cold water (238° F). Cool slightly, add the marshmallows, butter and vanilla and beat until creamy. Pour into buttered shallow pan to cool. Cut in squares.

Ice Cream Fudge

2 cups sugar
1½ cups milk

Butter size of walnut
½ teaspoon vanilla

Boil until a soft ball forms in cold water. When done, add ½ teaspoon vanilla and 2 tablespoons marshmallow cream. Beat steadily until thick. Pour into buttered pan to cool. Chopped nuts may be added, if desired.

Glacé Sugar for Nuts and Fruits

2 cups granulated sugar
2/3 cup boiling water

1/8 teaspoon cream of tartar

Boil sugar, water and cream of tartar until soft ball forms in cold water and is brittle and clear (310° F). Do not stir while cooking. If the sugar becomes too hard, add 1 tablespoon of water and cook and test again. Dip the prepared nuts and/or fruits in hot syrup using a candy dipper, being careful not to shake or stir the syrup. Lay on greased paper or plate to harden.

Potato Cocoanut Candy

1 medium potato
2 cups sifted con-
fectioners sugar
1 bar sweet chocolate

1 teaspoon vanilla
2 cups cocoanut
Juice of ½ orange

Cook the potato in boiling water then force through ricer. There should be ½ cup potato when done. Add to hot potato sugar, cocoanut, orange juice and vanilla, adding more sugar if necessary to make it stiff enough to handle. Pack solidly in 7-inch square pan, lined with waxed paper. Spread top with thin layer of melted sweet chocolate. Let stand several hours and cut in squares after turning out so that chocolate is on bottom.

Divinity Fudge

2 cups white sugar
½ cup white Karo
¼ cup water
Salt

1 cup walnut meats
1 teaspoon vanilla
1 egg white

Boil sugar, karo, water until soft ball forms in cold water. Add slowly to stiffly beaten egg white to which salt has been added. Beat. Add nuts and vanilla and pour into buttered pan to cool

Oatmeal Fudge

1 package light brown
sugar

¼ stick oleo
1/3 cup evaporated milk

Mix ingredients and put on medium heat to boil for 1 minute. Add tablespoon marshmallow fluff (about ½ jar of 7½ oz. size), then add 3 cups quick cooking oatmeal (dry), 2 teaspoons vanilla and nuts, if desired. Pour into buttered pan to cool.

Swiss Fudge

1 pound white chocolate
1 pound milk chocolate

¼ pound coconut oil

Melt white and milk chocolate in double boiler, add coconut oil and allow to cool until plastic texture. The add ½ pound pecans or walnuts and mix. Spread in buttered pan to cool.

Molasses Cocoanut Rolls

2 pounds old fashioned
  molasses
3¼ pounds desicatted
  cocoanut

3 pounds corn syrup
Salt to taste
Shredded cocoanut

Heat molasses to 180°, add coconut and mix thoroughly. Set aside and allow coconut to soften, then add corn syrup and salt, stir and cook until a soft ball is formed in cold water. Spread on greased cookie sheet to cool. Cut into desired shapes, moisten candies and roll in toasted coconut.

Fruit Bars

1 cup figs
1 cup dates

2 cups English walnut
  meats

Stem figs, stone dates, mix with nuts, and put through food chopper. Mix thoroughly and press firmly ¾ inch thick in buttered pan. Cut in squares or shape in balls. Roll in powdered sugar.

Sugared Almonds

½ pound almonds,
  blanched
1 cup sugar

1 teaspoon vanilla
½ teaspoon cinnamon
½ cup water

Cook sugar and water 5 minutes in heavy iron frying pan, add nuts and cook and stir until syrup begins to look white and slightly sugared. Add flavorings and set pan aside 10 minutes. Set over low heat on asbestos mat and stir constantly until sugar starts to melt. Pour on cake cooler over waxed paper. Separate to dry.

Peanut Brittle

1½ cups shelled, ray
  peanuts
¼ teaspoon salt
1 cup sugar

½ cup corn syrup
½ cup water
1½ tablespoons butter
½ teaspoon lemon extract

Sprinkle nuts with salt and warm in oven. Put sugar, corn syrup and water in pan, stir until it begins to boil, wash down sides with wet pastry brush, and cook to 295° F. or until mixture is very brittle when tried in cold water. Add butter, flavoring and nuts and pour into shallow buttered pan. As soon as it can be handled, turn the mass over and pull and stretch it out as thin as possible. Break into irregular pieces.

Peppermints

1½ cups sugar
½ cup boiling water

6 drops oil of peppermint

Put sugar and water in pan, stir until dissolved, boil until syrup spins long thread. Add flavoring, beat until creamy, and drop from tip of spoon on waxed paper. Reheat as mixture becomes too thick.

Wintergreen Wafers

1 teaspoon granulated gelatin
2 teaspoons cold water
Confectioners sugar

3 teaspoons boiling water
Few drops oil of wintergreen

Soak gelatin in cold water 5 minutes, dissolve in boiling water and strain. Add wintergreen and gradually sugar enough to knead. Roll very thin on board dredged with sugar. Shape with small, round cutter or cut in squares. Let stand until dry and brittle. For variety, color with vegetable coloring and flavor with vanilla, orange or lemon extract, clove or cinnamon.

BEVERAGES

Cranberry Holiday Punch

2 cups cranberry juice
  cocktail
1 cup orange juice
Juice of 2 lemons

½ cup pineapple juice
½ cup sugar
2 cups water

Mix ingredients in punch bowl and chill before serving.

Unfermented Grape Wine

Pick, stem and mash grapes, cool with as little water as for jelly. When soft, strain through bag. To 1 quart of juice add 1½ cups sugar. Cook until sugar is dissolved. While boiling hot, bottle and seal. Allow ⅓ juice to ⅔ water for a nice drink.

Hot Fruit Drink

2 quarts apple juice
2 cups cranberry juice
¾ gallon grape juice

3 sticks cinnamon
Pinch salt

Simmer 2-4 hours. Add water to taste. Makes 1½ gallons. Serve hot or cold.

Cranberry Cocktail

1 gallon water
5 cups sugar

2 quarts cranberries
Juice of 3 lemons

Boil sugar and water together. Add chopped cranberries and boil 3 minutes. Drain in jelly bag, add lemon juice when cool.

Honey Fruit Punch

Dissolve ½ cup honey in 2½ cups hot water. Add 2½ cups cold water and let mixture chill. Then add 4 cups orange juice, ½ cup lemon juice and 2½ cups grapefruit juice. Chill thoroughly and serve over chipped ice.

Chocolate Cream Nectar

2 squares chocolate (1 oz.)	1 cup sugar
½ cup liquid coffee	Whipped cream
3 cups water	1 teaspoon vanilla

Melt chocolate in a dry saucepan over gentle heat, add coffee liquid and cook 2 minutes, stirring constantly. Add sugar and water and cook 5 minutes. Chill, add vanilla and pour into glasses, each containing 1 tablespoon whipped cream. Chill before serving.

Hot Chocolate

2 squares chocolate
2 teaspoons sugar
3 cups milk

Whipped cream
4 tablespoons cold water
1 teaspoon vanilla

Put chocolate into saucepan or top of double boiler with water and sugar, cook over gentle heat until the chocolate is melted. Add milk gradually and bring to boiling point. Beat until foamy, flavor with vanilla and serve with spoonful of whipped cream on each cup.

Blackberry Cordial

1 quart blackberry juice
2 cups sugar
¼ teaspoon cloves
1 pint brandy

1 teaspoon nutmeg
1 teaspoon cinnamon
1 teaspoon all spice

Crush enough blackberries to give 1 quart of juice. Put in heavy saucepan with sugar, spices and cook 5 minutes. After it boils, skim and cover closely until cold. Strain, add brandy and bottle and seal.

Coffee Syrup

1½ quarts strong coffee   6 cups sugar

Make the coffee very strong; 1 pound coffee to 1¾ quarts of water. Clear and strain, combine with sugar and bring to boiling point. Jar hot in sterilized bottles. Use 2 tablespoons coffee syrup to ¾ cup milk.

Iced Coffee

Use 3 tablespoons of coffee syrup (see above) to 1 tablespoon cream and ¾ cup milk.

Varsity Punch

Juice of 8 oranges
1 cup lime juice
1 large can shredded
  pineapple

3 1/3 cups sugar
5 cups water
Ice water

Boil the sugar and water together for 10 minutes. Chill, pour over fruit and lime juices and let stand for 2 hours. Dilute to taste with ice water. Serves 40.

Pineapple Lemonade

2 cups hot water
1 cup sugar
4 cups ice water

1 can crushed pineapple
Juice of 3 lemons

Make a syrup by boiling sugar and water for 10 minutes. Cool. Add pineapple and lemon juice. Strain, add ice water and serve in lemonade glasses. Serves 16-20 glasses.

Raspberry or Loganberry Ade

1 quart can home preserved
    raspberries or logan-
    berries
Juice of 2 lemons

1 cup sugar
2 cups water
Ice water

Boil together sugar and water for 10 minutes. Cool, Add raspberry, which should be quite liquid, turn in lemon juice and let stand 2 hours to ripen. Dilute with ice water to desired strength and serve without straining.

Iced Tea

6 teaspoons tea
¼ cup syrup stock or

Sugar to taste
4 cups boiling water

Tea should be in crock or pitcher, pour over boiling water and let stand, covered for 5 minutes in a warm place. Strain on lemon and sweetening, stir and let cool. Serve with thin slice of lemon to each glass.

Cereal Coffee

3 pounds whole wheat
1 pound whole barley
1 cup ground chicary

3 tablespoons molasses
3 tablespoons butter

Roast the wheat and barley until brown, stirring often. When as dark as a coffee berry, add butter and molasses, stirring until it is absorbed and the grains separate. Remove from oven and when cold, add the chicary. Grind in a coffee mill. To make, use 2 tablespoons coffee to each person and 1¼ cups cold water. Boil 1 hour and serve with sugar and cream or milk.

Apple Sideup

¾ cup apple juice, chilled
¼ cup milk, chilled
1 egg

¼ teaspoon cinnamon
1 teaspoon honey

Combine all ingredients in shaker, blender, or mixing bowl. Shake or beat to a froth at low speed. Pour into tall glass. Serve immediately. Serves 1.

Tropic Nog

¾ cup milk, chilled
I egg

2 tablespoons frozen
orange-grapefruit juice

Combine in shaker, blender or mixing bowl. Shake or beat to a froth at low speed. Pour in tall glass. Serve immediately. Serves 1. (Glass may be garnished with rim of confectioners sugar.)

Eye Opener

I cup tomato or vegetable
juice, chilled
1/8 teaspoon salt

I egg
Dash tabasco
1/8 teaspoon Worcestershire

Combine in shaker, blender or mixing bowl at low speed. Shake to a froth and pour into tall glass. Serve immediately. Serves 1.

Gold Strike

1 cup orange juice,
chilled

1 tablespoon honey
1 egg

Combine in shaker, blender or mixing bowl and shake or beat to a froth at low speed. Pour into tall glass. Serve immediately. Serves 1. (May be garnished with cherry orange kabob.)

Coffee Cackle

1 cup milk, chilled
1 egg
1 teaspoon instant coffee

1 tablespoon maple
flavored syrup

Combine in shaker, blender or mixing bowl and shake or beat to froth at low speed. Pour in tall glass. Serve immediately. Serves 1.

Eggnog

1 egg, beaten slightly
¾ tablespoons sugar
Few grains salt
Few grains nutmeg

2/3 cup cold milk
1½ tablespoons sherry or
1 tablespoon brandy or
rum

Add sugar and salt to egg. Add liquor slowly, if used. Add milk gradually. Strain. Grate nutmeg over top. Serves 1.

Mulled Cider

1 quart cider
3/8 cup brown sugar
1 stick cinnamon (3 inches)

2 whole allspice
2 whole cloves

Boil cider and spices 5 minutes, remove spice bag and add sugar, boil 5 minutes. Serve hot. This may be prepared and kept hot over hot water until time for serving. Serves 6.

Fruit Punch with Whipped Cream

1 pint grape juice	Grated rind of 1 orange
3 tablespoons lemon juice	4 sprigs fresh mint
1/3 cup orange juice	Few grains salt
1 cup fresh pineapple	Few gratings nutmeg
pulp with juice	Crushed ice
¾ cup loaf sugar	1 pint bottle soda water
Grated rind of 1 lemon	Whipped cream

Mix fruit juices. Add sugar, which has been rubbed over lemon and orange. Add mint, salt and nutmeg. Cover and let stand in refrigerator 1 hour to ripen. Pour over crushed ice, add soda water, and serve in tall glasses with whipped cream on top. Garnish with mint leaves. Serves 10.

Rhubarb Punch

1½ pounds rhubarb	4 tablespoons lemon juice
1 quart water	Few grains salt
1½ cups sugar	Crushed ice
1/3 cup orange juice	Charged water or ginger ale

Cut rhubarb in small pieces; there should be 1 quart. Add water and cook until fruit is soft. Squeeze through double thickness of cheesecloth, add sugar, stir until sugar is dissolved, bring to boiling point, add fruit juices and salt. Bottle, or chill and serve with crushed ice and an equal amount of charged water or ginger ale. Serves 12.

Mint Tulip

1 bunch fresh mint	1 cup lemon juice
1½ cups sugar	3 pints ginger ale
½ cup water	Ice

Add mint leaves, sugar and water to lemon juice. Let stand 30 minutes. Pour over a large piece of ice and add ginger ale. Serves 10.

Club Punch

1 cup water	1 quart Vichy
2 cups sugar	3 sliced oranges
1 quart Burgundy	½ cup crushed pineapple
1 cup rum	Juice of 2 lemons
1/3 cup brandy	1 cup tea infusion
1/3 cup Benedictine	Ice

Boil sugar and water 10 minutes. Mix other ingredients (except ice), sweeten to taste with syrup and pour over block of ice in punch bowl. Serves 24.

THE ABUNDANT WATERS

Each year millions of dollars of lobster, fish and shellfish are taken from Maine's waters. The Indians have an interesting folklore as to how these fish really came into being.

Ages ago, a tribe of Indians had a village on the bank of a sparkling brook in the Maine woods. Suddenly the brook became as dry as "a dead bone in the ashes of a warm fire." The tribe suffered, and so the bravest Indian was sent to discover the reason why there was no water. Up stream he found a huge dam with a pond on which stood another Indian village ruled by a sagamore of frightful aspect. The brave returned to his village and the drought continued. So, the men of the village prepared to destroy the tribe, break down the dam and have pure water.

Just then came Glooskap, ten feet high with a hundred feathers in his scalp-lock, painted face and a clam shell hanging from each ear. He heard the story of the drought and proceeded up the stream to the village at the great dam. The rude sagamore in the language of the Indians of the day, told Glooskap to "beat it." But the lord of all creatures, liking not such language, rose high as a pine tree and seizing the chief, hurled him into the pond. And he became a frog.

The awful magic transformed the village. Some of the Indians were changed into leeches, others into crabs, lobsters, and fishes. Thus were created all the dwellers of the lakes and sea. The great Spirit broke down the dam and a great river began to flow to every quarter of the globe. And there they are today, the awful reminder of Glooskap's vengence. This legend must be true, for today lobsters, crabs and all manner of fish are to be found in the seven seas.

GUIDES TO

BETTER

COOKING

GUIDES TO BETTER COOKING

COOKERY TERMS TO KNOW

A la king   Food prepared in a rich cream sauce.

A la mode   "In the manner of." For desserts, it means "with ice cream."

Aspic   Clear, savory jelly used in molds to garnish cold dishes; made with gelatin or from meat bones, etc.

Au gratin   French term meaning a creamed dish with broiler-browned or oven-browned topping of buttered crumbs or crumbs-and-cheese.

Bake   To cook by dry heat in oven.

Barbecue   To broil or roast on grill or spit over coals or other heat. To cook with highly spiced sauce. Also means the picnic or meal of barbecued foods.

Baste   To drip or spoon fat or liquid of pan juices over food which is roasting, broiling, etc.

Batter   Semi-liquid mixture of flour, water, milk, eggs, etc. A coating for food to be fried. A cake, waffle or pancake mixture before baking.

Beat   To blend or whip with spoon, rotary hand beater, or electric mixer to combine foods or to incorporate air, as in egg whites.

Bind   To make a mixture hold together by adding liquid, beaten eggs, cream, etc.

Bisque   Thick cream soup. Also frozen cream dessert.

Blanch   To steep nuts, fruits, etc., in hot or boiling water to loosen skins for removing. Also, to reduce strong flavors or color of foods by immersing briefly in water at boiling point, off the fire.

GUIDES TO BETTER COOKING

COOKERY TERMS TO KNOW

A la king   Food prepared in a rich cream sauce.

A la mode   "In the manner of." For desserts, it means "with ice cream."

Aspic   Clear, savory jelly used in molds to garnish cold dishes; made with gelatin or from meat bones, etc.

Au gratin   French term meaning a creamed dish with broiler-browned or oven-browned topping of buttered crumbs or crumbs-and-cheese.

Bake   To cook by dry heat in oven.

Barbecue   To broil or roast on grill or spit over coals or other heat. To cook with highly spiced sauce. Also means the picnic or meal of barbecued foods.

Baste   To drip or spoon fat or liquid of pan juices over food which is roasting, broiling, etc.

Batter   Semi-liquid mixture of flour, water, milk, eggs, etc. A coating for food to be fried. A cake, waffle or pancake mixture before baking.

Beat   To blend or whip with spoon, rotary hand beater, or electric mixer to combine foods or to incorporate air, as in egg whites.

Bind   To make a mixture hold together by adding liquid, beaten eggs, cream, etc.

Bisque   Thick cream soup. Also frozen cream dessert.

Blanch   To steep nuts, fruits, etc., in hot or boiling water to loosen skins for removing. Also, to reduce strong flavors or color of foods by immersing briefly in water at boiling point, off the fire.

GUIDES TO BETTER COOKING

Blaze   To pour warmed brandy or liqueur over food and ignite.

Blend   To combine ingredients, mixing until smooth.

Boil   To cook in liquid at boiling temperature, when bubbles break the surface.

Bouillon   A clear, strained soup of stock made from beef veal or fowl cooked with seasoning and vegetables.

Braise   To brown in fat gently, with small amount of liquid added. Pan is covered to preserve juices.

Bread   To roll cutlet, croquettes, or other foods in crumbs.

Broil   To cook over or under direct heat.

Brown   To cook in a little fat at high heat until brown, sealing juices in; to place under broiler heat, or in oven, to brown top, as casserole or au gratin dishes.

Capers   Flower buds from shrub (also from nasturtiums) preserved in vinegar, used as condiment and in sauces. Usually imported in bottles.

Chop   To cut into small pieces with chopper or knife.

Coat   To dip in flour, crumbs, other mixtures before frying.

Consomme   Clarified bouillon or stock.

Cream   To work or beat shortening, butter, other fats until light and airy, with or without adding sugar, or flour, etc.

Cube   To cut into small square pieces.

GUIDES TO BETTER COOKING

Cut and fold To blend mixture with liquid by first turning spoon sideways in a cutting motion as the two are combined, then lifting mixture from bottom and folding over top with spoon until all is mixed.

Dice Cut in small squares.

Dilute To thin by adding liquid. To diminish strength or flavor of liquid.

Drain To strain liquid from solid food.

Filter To strain liquid through several thicknesses of cheesecloth or a special paper filter.

Flake To separate chunks of fish, other foods, lightly into thin pieces with fork.

Fold To lift mixture with spoon in an overlapping motion from one side of bowl to the other.

French Fry To cook in deep hot fat until brown and crisp.

Fricassee To cook by braising with slightly more liquid than in braising. This is usually chicken or veal stewed in cream sauce, with seasoning and white wine added, or in brown sauce or stock.

Garnish To decorate a dish.

Glaze Coating of syrup, gelatin or aspic for hams, roast chicken, etc. Also, brown particles left in pan in which meat or poultry roasted. Also means to brown the top sauce which has been poured over a dish set under broiler or in oven.

Grate To reduce foods to small particles by rubbing over grater or using a grinder-grater.

GUIDES TO BETTER COOKING

Knead To work dough with the hands, using a folding and pressing motion until it is smooth and spongy.

Leaven To lighten a mixture by adding yeast, baking powder, eggs.

Liquor Liquid from shellfish. Liquid from food as it cooks.

Marinade Mixture of seasoned liquids in which food is soaked to tenderize or add flavor.

Mill To beat to a froth with a whisk beater, as in the preparation of hot chocolate and other milk drinks. Also, small mixers, choppers and similar devices are called mills.

Mince To chop finely or put through chopper. Also means the resulting food mixture from such chopping.

Mould, or mold To shape gelatin-stiffened mixture, or ice cream or other dessert.

Mull To heat beverages, such as cider or wine, with sugar and spices; should be slow heat to bring out flavors.

Pan Broil To cook uncovered in skillet with little or no fat pouring off fat as it emerges.

Parboil To boil a few minutes, or until partially cooked, in preparation for next step of recipe.

Pare Also peel. To remove skin of fruit and vegetables with knife or parer.

Pickle To preserve in brine or vinegar. Also pickled vegetables and fruits.

GUIDES TO BETTER COOKING

Pit To remove kernel of fruit.

Render To cook or heat meat until the fat liquefies and can be drained off.

Saute To brown quickly in small amount of oil or fat.

Scald To pour boiling water over food. To heat liquid, such as milk, to just under boiling temperature when tiny bubbles start to form around edge.

Scallop To bake in cream sauce topped with crumbs or crumbs-and-cheese. Also a shellfish.

Sear To brown surface of meat at high temperature to hold juices in.

Shred To slice in small strips.

Sift To shake dry ingredients, such as flour, seasonings, baking powder together in a sieve or special sifter.

Simmer To cook in liquid below boiling point. Liquid should move gently, with bubbles forming below surface.

Singe To burn off the down or hairs from plucked game or fowl over a flame.

Skim To remove fat and other floating matter from surface of cooking liquid with spoon, strainer spoon or skimmer.

Steep To heat food in water, below boiling point, to extract juices, flavor, color.

Stew Cook in liquid, at slow boiling.

GUIDES TO BETTER COOKING

Stock   Liquid strained from cooked meat, fish, poultry, vegetables.

Tenderize   Marinate pound use commercial tenderizer on meat.

Thicken   Flour, cornstarch, potato starch, cream, egg added to mixtures to give more body.

Truss   Method of preparing dressed chicken or other fowl for roasting pan. Tie wings and legs of bird to body by skewers and string so bird holds shape during roasting.

GUIDES TO BETTER COOKING

EQUIVALENT MEASURES

Butter or Margarine .... 1 ounce equals 2 tablespoons fat.

¼ pound equals ½ cup fat (or 1 stick)

½ pound equals 1 cup fat

1 pound equals 2 cups fat

Cheese — American .... 1 pound equals 5 cups grated

Cream (3 oz.) .... 1 package equals 6⅔ tablespoons

Chocolate .... 1 square equals 1 ounce
equals 3½ tablespoons dry cocoa
plus 1 tablespoon butter

Crumbs — saltine crackers .... 7 coarsely crumbled equal
1 cup (9 finely crumbled)

graham crackers .... 9 coarsely crumbled equal
1 cup (11 finely crumbled)

small vanilla wafers 20 coarsely crumbled equal
1 cup (30 finely crumbled)

zwieback .... 4 coarsely crumbled equal 1
cup (9 finely crumbled)

Eggs .... 12 to 14 egg yolks equal 1 cup
8 to 10 egg whites equal 1 cup

Flours — all-purpose .... 1 pound sifted equals 4 cups

cake .... 1 pound sifted equals 4½ cups

graham .... 1 pound unsifted equals 3½ cups

corn meal .... 1 pound equals 3 cups

GUIDES TO BETTER COOKING

Fruits and nuts .... 1 lemon equals 3 to 4
tablespoons juice

1 orange equals 6 to 8
tablespoons juice

1 package seedless raisins
equals 3 cups (15-ounce)

¼ pound shelled nuts
equals 1 cup chopped

Rice .... 1 pound equals 2⅓ cups raw rice

Sugar — granulated .... 1 pound equals 2¼ cups

brown, firmly packed .. 1 pound equals 2¼ cups

confectioners' .... 1 pound equals 3½ cups

IN APPRECIATION

Outside contributors of some recipes —

American Dairy Association
Chicago, Illinois

Blue Cheese-Bologna Wedges
Cheese Log
Surprise Dip
Green Pepper Cheese Broil
Deviled Deckers
Blue Cheese Nut Balls
Ham Loaf Supreme
Meat Balls in Sour Cream Sauce
Meat Loaf Ring
Butter Baked Turkey
Butter Sauce for Vegetables
Butter Pecan Squash Casserole
Pimiento Buttered Celery and Peas
Majestic Broccoli Mold
Ring Around Hash Dinner
Gingerbread Men
Holiday Yeast Cookies
Press Cookies
Christmas Cut-outs
Cherry Jewels
Pinwheel Cookies

Bethel Inn
Bethel, Maine

Baked Stuffed Pork Chops
Boiled Round of Beef
Swedish Meat Balls — Family Style
Braised Short Ribs of Beef
Yankee Beef Stew

Boone's Custom House Wharf
Portland, Maine

Tuna Chowder
Fish Chowder for 6
Shrimp Chowder
Lobster Salad
Cranberry Salad
Downeast Shrimp Salad
Hot Crabmeat Salad
Swordfish Salad Mold
Sailors Salad
Lobster A La Newburg
Baked Lobster with Clam Dressing
Lobster Thermidore
Lobster Delight
Scalloped Lobster
Lobster Wiggle
Maine Lobster Casserole A Gratin
Lobster Bisque
Shrimp and Cauliflower Casserole
Deviled Shrimp Casserole

Shrimp Wiggle
Roast Saddle of Venison with
    Mint Sauce
Shepherds Pie
Maine Coast Clam Fritters
Scalloped Clams
Maine Clam Pie
New England Salt Fish Dinner
Cheese-Fish Casserole
Baked Scallops
Scallop Casserole
Baked Stuffed Fish Fillets
Crab Loaf
Stuffed Maine Potatoes
Queen Victoria Johnny Cake
Apple Muffins
Maine Brown Bread
Downeast Beef and Potato Pie
Stew Beef with Dumplings

Len Libby's Candy Shops
Portland, Scarborough,
South Portland, Maine

Molasses Cocoanut Rolls
Swiss Fudge

Marco's Italian Restaurant
Lewiston, Maine

Beef Strogonoff
Veal Scalopini

Wm. Underwood Co.
Boston, Mass.

New England Baked Beans
'n Franks

Bordens, Inc., Food Div.
Snow Food Products

Old Fashioned Corn-Clam Chowder
Creamed Shrimp,
    New England Style
Browned Clam Hash
Chessy Clam Casserole
Clams Poulette
Creamed Clams
Clams Supreme
Clam Souffle with Shrimp
    Newburg Sauce
Clam Tetrazzini
Deep Dish Clam and
    Cornbread Pie
Macaroni and Cheese

**Poultry and Egg
National Board
Chicago, Illinois**

Soft Cooked Eggs
Hard Cooked Eggs
Fried Eggs
Broiled Eggs
Baked Eggs
Poached Eggs
Scrambled Eggs
Creamed Eggs Remekin's
Barbecued Omelet
French or Plain Omelet
Herb Omelet
Puffy Omelet
Fruit Omelet
Ten Minute Omelet
Spanish Omelet
Noodle Omelet
Poultry or Meat Omelet
Seafood Omelet
Mushroom-Cheese Omelet

**Department of Sea & Shore Fisheries
Augusta, Maine**

Whiting Salad
Broiled State of Maine Lobster
Baked State of Maine Lobster
Lobster Roll
Lobster Casserole
Tangy Maine Lobster
Shrimp Newburg
Deviled Shrimp En Coquille
Adelaide's Shrimp Gumbo
Shrimp Divan
Shrimp Sandwich Filling
Maine Shrimp Pate
Beulah's Shrimp Bake
Shrimp and Deviled Egg Casserole
Boiled Maine Shrimp
Shrimp Stuffed Peppers
Jambelayah, Maine Style
Baked Maine Shrimp Cheese Puffs
Baked Shrimp
Curried Shrimp
Mary Ann's Clam Casserole
Maine Steamed Clams
Maine Clam Casserole

Maine Sea-Burgers
Fried Clams
Scalloped Mussels
Panned Mussels
Mussels on the Half Shell
Turban of Fish
Baked Stuffed Haddock
Baked Creamed Haddock Filets
Sweet and Sour Mackerel
Pollock Filet with Dressing
Cusk Pie
Baked Halibut Steak with Cheese
Whiting Dinner Casserole
Maine Whiting with Mushrooms
Hake Casserole
Baked Ocean Perch
Filet of Sole Marjuery
Sardines with State of Maine Sauce
Halibut-Lobster Casserole

**Bureau of Commercial Fisheries
Marine Sardine Council
Washington, D.C.**

Maine Sardine Cole Slaw
Maine Sardine Cocktail, Machias
Maine Sardine Casserole Caliente
Fisherman's Bake
Cheese Baked Maine Sardines
   and Pasta

**Department of Agriculture
Augusta, Maine**

Blushing Hawaiian Chicken
Maine Chicken A-La-Jet
Skillet Chicken
Potato Chip Chicken
Maine-ly Chicken Casserole
Chicken Newburg
Mashed Potato Bake
Oven Brown Potatoes
Baked Potatoes
Parslied Potatoes
Spider Spuds
Famous Potato Salad
Ma's Scalloped Potatoes
Bacon French Fries Bake
Patio Potatoes Anne
Skillet Potato Salad
Blueberry Muffins

INDEX

NOTES

NOTES

NOTES